THE JIMMY RANEY BOOK

A COMPLETE STUDY OF MELODIC LINE

BY JIMMY RANEY & JON RANEY

©2024 Sher Music Co., P.O. Box 445, Petaluma, CA, 94953 All Rights Reserved.
International Copyright Secured.
Made in the U.S.A. No part of this book may be reproduced in any form
without written permission from the publisher.
Design and layout by Jon Raney and Linda McLaughlin.
ISBN 978-1-883217-85-3

ABOUT THE ARTIST

JIMMY RANEY was born in 1927 in Louisville, KY. He began guitar at age ten, working professionally by his teens, then moving to Chicago to pursue a jazz career. Big band stints with Jerry Wald (1944), Woody Herman (1948) and Artie Shaw (1949) followed, making his first known recordings with Al Haig in 1948. By the '50s, he had joined forces with Stan Getz, recording the famous 1951 Storyville sessions and then his debut record, *Jimmy Raney Plays* in 1953.

He studied composition with Hall Overton, joined the Red Norvo trio and won *Downbeat*'s Best Jazz Guitarist polls in 1954 and 1955. Records for Paramount and Prestige followed, with Bob Brookmeyer, Al Cohn, Hank Jones, and Jim Hall, among others. In the '60s, he made many recordings as a sideman (with Gary McFarland, Dave Pike, Lalo Schifrin, and others) then released the outstanding, *Two Jims and Zoot* (Jim Hall and Zoot Sims) in 1964. However, by the mid-sixties, his increasing alcoholism almost ended his career.

Jimmy made a comeback in the 1970s, making records with Al Haig, Billy Higgins, Sam Jones, and other greats. In 1976, his classic, *Live in Tokyo* trio album was released. He toured with son, Doug in the '70s and '80s, making 4 records (*Stolen Moments, Duets, Raney '81* and *Nardis*). Three Criss Cross records followed until his final album as a leader, *But Beautiful* (1990). While his worsening Meniere's disease made public performance near impossible, he did teach and write. In late 1993, a stroke left him completely paralyzed and he eventually passed away in May of 1995.

The quick biography above is for those who may not be familiar with the life and work of Jimmy Raney. For those who are (including acclaimed musicians), his frequent omission from jazz guitar history can be a little confounding. The purpose of this book, in part, is to correct this and bring Jimmy's often overlooked musical achievements into proper perspective, as he is clearly among the very best jazz musicians ever.

(Section III, continued)

- D: Major Chord concepts ... 59
- E: Minor Chord Concepts ... 64
  - Minor Moving 7th ... 64
  - 5-123 Scalar Phrase ... 65
  - 5-6-7-1 ... 66
  - Polyrhythmic Minor Scales ... 66
- F: Dominant Chord Concepts ... 67
  - ½ W Diminished ... 67
    - a. ♭9♯9 Combo ... 67
    - b. Upper Structure VI Triad (V13♭9) ... 69
    - c. Upper Structure ♭V Triad (V7♭9♭5) ... 70
    - d. Upper Structure ♯IIm7 (♭IIIm7) ... 70
    - e. Sequence and Scale Patterns ... 71
  - Altered Dominant ... 72
    - a. The "Descending Altered Lick" ... 72
    - b. The "Barney Kessel lick" ... 73
  - ♭vi-♭II7 Substitution ... 74
  - V7 Substitutes: Diminished and Non-V7 Polychords ... 77

Exercises: Chapter 8D-F
Major, Minor and Dominant Chords ... 79

Chapter 9: Compositional, Development and Phrasing Concepts ... 82
- A. Diminution ... 82
- B. Set-up phrases ... 83
- C. Asymmetrical Joins ... 88

Exercises: Chapter 9A-C:
Diminution, Set-ups, and Asymmetrical Joins ... 92
- D. "Evolving" Sequence & Expansion ... 95
- E. Thematic Contrasts & Repetition ... 97
- F. The "Undercurrent of Three" ... 101

Exercises: Chapter 9D-F
Evolving Sequence, Thematic Contrast & "Undercurrent of Three" ... 104
- G: Question and Answer ... 105
- H: "Drawing the Harmony" ... 110
- I: De-emphasizing Beat 1 ... 112
  - Beat 4 Placement ... 112
  - Beat 3 Placement ... 114
  - Beat 2 Placement ... 116

Exercises: Chapter 9G-I:
Question/Answer, Harmonic Drawing, Weak Beat Emphasis ... 117

Chapter 10: The Raney Approach — Creating a Complete Solo ... 118

Chapter 11: Additional Solo Studies & Exercises ... 122

TABLE OF CONTENTS

About the Artist ii
Jimmy Raney's Original Introduction iii
Preface iv
Acknowledgments vi
Table of Contents vii

SECTION I:
Jimmy Raney's Improvised Line 1

   Chapter 1: Constructing and Editing Jazz Lines 2
      Things To Think About 6
   Chapter 2: Refining / Enhancing Lines with Rhythmic Devices 7
      Polyrhythm 8
      Harmonic Dislocation 9
      Solo Analysis 11
      Things To Think About 13
   Chapter 3: Sequence & Development of Line 14
      Things To Think About 17
   Chapter 4: Intervallic and Directional Variety in Line 18
      Things to Think About 21

SECTION II:
• Background/History • Concepts in Recordings 22

   Chapter 5: Jimmy Raney's Polyrhythmic Devices in Recordings . . 23
      Background/History 23
      Polyrhythmic Scale Patterns 24
      Polyrhythmic Arpeggio Patterns 25
      Polyrhythmic General Phrase Patterns 27
      Polyrhythmic Blues Lick Patterns 28
      Things To Think About 31
   Chapter 6: Jimmy Raney's Displacement Concepts in Recordings . . 32
      Harmonic Dislocation 32
      Add/Subtract Concepts 34
      Free (unresolved) Displacement 35
   Chapter 7: Jimmy Raney's Advanced Asymmetry & Polymetrics in Recordings 38
      Concepts in Practice 38
      Parker's Influence on Jimmy Raney's Dislocation/Polymetric Concept 39
      Things To Think About 43

SECTION III:
Primer and Practice on the Elements of Jimmy Raney's Language 45

   Chapter 8: The Essential Elements of Jimmy Raney's Phrases 47
      A: The II-V Licks 47
      B: Inverted Chord Lines 49
      C: Auxiliary Tones and Melodic Intervals 51
         Passing Tones (PT) 51
         Neighbor Tones (NT) 53
         Turns 53
         Multiple NT & PT licks 54

   Exercises: Chapter 8A-C
   II-V's, Inverted Chords, Auxiliary Tones 58

ACKNOWLEDGMENTS

I would like to acknowledge the following people in helping this twenty-plus year unfinished project finally to a successful result:

Ed Fuqua, for introducing me and this book to Chuck Sher (a hell of a nice guy, I might add).

Stephen (Ephraim) Schwab for his constant encouragement of my ideas and my talents generally, often when others look past me.

Jamey Aebersold, for reinforcing the value of this work, when I had lost faith.

Jeff Brent, who helped me proof-read this lengthy treatise and offered helpful suggestions.

Nikhil Hogan, for re-sparking my interest in this book.

My wife, Yajaira and my daughter Talia, for their unwavering love and support.

And finally, to Jimmy Raney, without whom, of course this book would never exist. He continues to speak to all of us through his music, videos, writings, and words well beyond his passing, providing once-in-a-lifetime insights into this difficult thing called improvisation.

Long live the legend of Jimmy Raney!

The first 2 chapters of the book, except for a few minor editorial updates, section titles and ending adds, are essentially my father's work intact from his original manuscript (and mostly in first-person as the author). The practice exercises and solos he wrote out were moved to the final chapters, along with my own. Chapters 3-4 reflect my intermingling of his materials with other materials sourced from his workshops and a widely circulated audio lesson from the '80s where he quoted his own published instruction materials. Chapter 5 onward is entirely new material.

Jimmy's methodology for the initial part of the book is what one could term a "Socratic method." Essentially you have a musical line, begin a process of self-questioning to improve it, and once the answers are hashed out, implement the changes necessary to bring about the best result.

My methodology in Section II was to introduce his recorded output to the mix and organize those recordings thematically, but also echoing and amplifying his original chapters. As with his original work, my emphasis clearly was on his unique contributions to the jazz art, and particularly his innovations in rhythm.

Section III reflects a desire to "workshop" the nuts and bolts of my father's language. This was clearly the hardest part of the book as it really demanded a thorough knowledge of his recorded materials and thinking process (as well as could be expected given his passing nearly 17 years earlier). At different points I had to think of novel concepts and even invent musical definitions that helped explain his methods better.

The final practice chapters reflect trying to solve the quandary that we all face regarding studying the masters: How do you copy their work and still speak with your own voice? For example, how do you avoid playing their solos verbatim for a chorus, but then following up with your own ideas that are not as well thought out or related?

I hope you find the concepts discussed in this book both unique and enlightening as it was for me in the discovery process. Like you I'm still a humble student of the process and my father's genius. It may very well take a few attempts to get through the entire book and you may need to focus on certain sections for an extended period or set them aside and come back to them. Don't give up! I think you will enjoy this unique exploration into Jimmy Raney's contribution to this unique art form we call, for lack of a better word, *jazz*.

JON RANEY
2024, NYC

PREFACE

In 1985, I spent 6 months in Louisville living with my father. I was a fresh music graduate from Hunter College, and Dad and I had a lot to discuss about music generally. We talked about Beethoven, Mozart, ran through scores together and had debates about various musicians and musical periods. But when it came to jazz, I was not near where I needed to be as a professional musician, so my father did his best to get me more practical experience and advice on improvement. And he was in a place at that point where he was interested in teaching and putting things that he was teaching students down to paper.

He was already nearly finished with the book started a few years before, but he still was pasting together his xeroxed (yes, I said Xerox) manuscripts and snippets and hand-written notes. He was quite excited about it as was I. Most books of the day were the typical things you'd see that taught scales, chords, and licks ad nauseum. However, this book was not at all like that and dealt with his very personal compositional process of constructing line which, as we all know, Dad had few peers. Although perhaps somewhat short in length (approximately 31 pages including the intro), at least it could serve as a working manuscript to the publisher he forwarded to, Mel Bay. PLUS, he also had a few jazz books already selling with Jamey Aebersold.

Sadly, this wasn't to be as Mel Bay declined and Dad just didn't pursue this further. I'm sure it stung a little, but he moved on. A short 10 years later my father passed on. Among many of his belongings left to me were his pictures, cassettes, writings, and this book, though I did nothing with it until after I began blogging in 2006. Given the advances in technology, I began transcribing what he had written to Microsoft Word pulling in the musical examples with musical notation software.

In transcribing to the digital version, the original number of handwritten manuscript pages shrunk substantially. Additionally, though brilliant, the work still had an unfinished quality to it, with certain things like chapter definitions, section titling, chapter end practice, and other things typical of the burgeoning standard for jazz instruction books. I also felt that more samples of his own recorded performances would not only round out the book but might also demonstrate his line concepts even better. I surmised that I just needed to flesh out more recordings, organize them into little concept buckets and then build logically around the core work, with annotations and appraisals of the excerpts. But as I woodshed his recordings, the work grew further, eventually adding wholly new original analysis, theory, and exercises of my own.

At the time, my decision to do this might've been the boldest but also perhaps the most ill-advised thing I could've done, as this revised and updated book would stay on the shelf after 2012. Essentially, I looked at the roughly 112 pages I came up with and suddenly didn't convince me and I just lost the mojo to finish it. I had let a few friends see the copy, but I found only one person that could truly digest it. I released a small portion of the book on my blog to give readers a taste. There may be a few of Dad's students that were given copies of the original manuscript during their lessons as well.

I would not pursue this book again until an Internet Radio personality, Nikhil Hogan, interviewed me in March of 2021 and had many questions about some things I posted from the book. He had little knowledge of the backstory behind it. Suddenly I had a renewed belief in the value of the work, given Nikhil's enthusiasm for the little bit he had seen. I gave it a shot and made a final push to finish, and the results are what you see here.

JIMMY RANEY'S ORIGINAL INTRODUCTION

Jazz improvisation is by now a recognized American art form taking its place alongside European concert music. One of the most attractive and compelling aspects of jazz, aside from its individual sound and character, is the fact that it is improvised. I was originally attracted to it for this reason.

"Classical" or concert music was at one time partly improvised. During the Baroque period, keyboard players had to improvise an accompaniment from a figured bass. This is very similar to our practice of "comping" from a set of chord symbols. Also, some of the great composer-performers, J.S. Bach being the supreme example, were consummate improvisors. He was capable of improvising three, four and five-part fugues from a given theme.

Beethoven also was renowned for his improvising. Improvising pieces being a regular part of many of his concert performances. These practices faded away during the 19th century. Until now it has disappeared completely. The joy of improvising is a very pleasurable and satisfying experience that is not duplicated by either composing with pencil and paper or performing composed music. This gap in present day concert music is now filled by jazz.

How do we teach jazz? Where do we go to learn it? You must learn it from the people who can play it. Since there are few good teacher-players available in many areas, this poses a problem. If there are not any in your area, consider going to some other city to seek them out. Nowadays many universities have jazz programs with good jazz teachers. Buying and studying the recordings of the great jazz players is the traditional way and still perhaps one of the best ways to learn.

Last, but not least, you must get together and play with other players in order to get the "feel" of playing. There are also many good play-along records now available. These are a useful adjunct and substitute.

This book deals primarily with methods of constructing good and interesting lines. There are also duets and solos for practice and study.

JIMMY RANEY
1986, Louisville, KY

SECTION I
JIMMY RANEY'S IMPROVISED LINE

CHAPTER 1: CONSTRUCTING AND EDITING JAZZ LINES

I will begin by constructing lines and then analyzing and rebuilding them. For this purpose, I will use three variations, (A, B and C) of the common four-measure I VI II V chord progression found in many standards.

Original:

Chord variations A, B & C:

A.

B.

C.

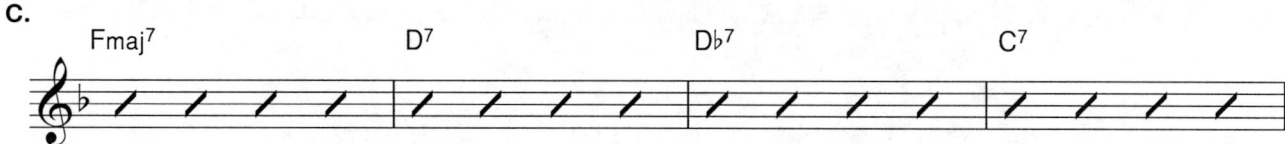

Let us construct a melodic line on the first chord variation, A:

Fig. A1

As we look this melodic line in Fig. A1, what are the strong and weak points of its construction? In its favor, it is a very song-like melody. It also fits the chords without "running" them and is sequential, which gives it coherence. But it is very monotonous because it repeats the same rhythm exactly. Let us see if we can fix some of the difficulty (see Fig. A2):

Fig. A2

Now the phrase has been filled in with added syncopation (dotted quarter and eighth in the first bar), added sequence in the second bar, and finally harmonic interest with a D♭ major seventh arpeggio on the first two beats of the third bar. Much of the original sequence remains, thereby retaining its original strength and coherence, but the monotony has been lessened by the alterations.

Let's try another variation:

Fig. A3

This is still related to the original Fig. A1 but has undergone further transformation. There are now ascending and descending scale sequences in bars 1 and 2. The phrase still pivots around the note common to all 4 chords, the C natural.

Let's try a new phrase on the harmonic progression of B, which substitutes dominant chords for the minors on VI and II:

Fig. B1

This is a pleasing phrase although rather simple. Let us add a couple of flatted 9ths and other alterations to give it more interest (see Fig. B2)

Fig. B2

In the first bar we have created syncopation by anticipating and holding the D. We have added flatted ninths on the D7, G7 and C7 chords. Note also the chromatic ascension from the 5th of the chord to the third of the next chord in bars 3 and 4. This gives a strong harmonic movement to the phrase as the third clearly defines the chord.

However, there is still not enough rhythmic interest here. Let us add more syncopation in measures 2, 3 and 4 by attacking the upbeats of the "and" of two and four and holding them over (see Fig. B3):

Fig. B3

Note also how both the ♭9 and ♯9 (D♭, E♭) were used as suspensions to the C in the fourth measure.

The next two examples further illustrate this altered suspension approach. In Fig. B4 measure 2, a natural 9th is paired with the root on chords D7, G7 and C7. Compare and contrast this with Fig. B5 where ♭9 and ♯9 suspensions are used on the same chords. Although the phrases are nearly identical, the altered 9th suspensions in Fig. B5 create a stronger pull towards resolution than in Fig. B4.

Fig. B4

Fig. B5

The next examples are over the C progression, which swap D♭7 for G7 (see Fig. C1).

Fig. C1

This phrase doesn't quite sound right. The flatted notes on the D♭7 phrase, although agreeing with D♭7, seem more out of key because they are unprepared and do not resolve to diatonic notes. Contrast this with the ♭9 and ♯9 notes used on the D7 and C7 chords. Although they include chromatic tones (E♭, D♭) they still resolve smoothly to the diatonic notes within the key of F (D and C respectively).

Interestingly, reversing the procedure does not help. In Fig. C2, diatonic ninths are used on the D7 and C7 chords and the ♭9 ♯9 combo is used on the D♭7. It sounds odd:

Fig. C2

Since neither D♭7 type tones nor diatonic ♭9/♯9 suspensions that resolve to D♭ seem to have worked well so far, let's try another solution: bitonality. In this case we will approach the chord melodically as if it were a G7 (as in prior examples) but against the D♭7 chord. This is simply a tritone substitution (see Fig. C3)

Fig. C3

Clearly this solution is much more melodic than the previous because the G7 is closer in key to F.

THINGS TO THINK ABOUT

- Use sequence with varied rhythm, and include pitches that create harmonic interest. (A1-A2)
- Vary the shape of the line. (A2, bar 3)
- Use flatted 9ths to create more melodic interest on dominant chords. (B2)
- Connect to the 3rds of the chords to better define the harmony. (B2)
- Use syncopation to sustain rhythmic vitality in the line. (B3)
- Use the ♭9 #9 suspension combination to create tension and resolution to the dominant root. (B5)
- Take special care preparing and resolving chromatic tones, resolving to diatonic key related pitches. (A3, C1-C3)

CHAPTER 2: REFINING / ENHANCING LINES WITH RHYTHMIC DEVICES

Long lines are part and parcel of modern jazz playing. Although anyone can play long lines, it is easy to fall prey to monotony without interesting rhythms. The lines to be discussed are more or less continuous, but are nevertheless successful because they contain rhythmic complexities, which create tension and sustain interest.

Earlier styles consisted of shorter phrases such as those of the Dixieland or the Swing era as exemplified by the phrase below:

Fig. 2-1

Let's now construct a longer phrase based on this:

Fig. 2-2

What's wrong with this revision? The syncopations that gave the previous line its life and vitality have been removed. It is harmonically and melodically similar to the first example, but it is rhythmically equivalent to the following rather dull phrase:

Fig. 2-3

Polyrhythm

One way to counteract rhythmic flatness in long lines is through the use of polyrhythmic phrases against the given meter.

Polyrhythms can be created by accents:

Fig. 2-4a

Or by groupings in scale sequences (b) or broken chord sequences (c).

b.

c.

In b and c, the accents are built into the phrases.

This sample phrase is similar to Fig. 2-2 but it utilizes 3/8-meter scale groupings, creating more rhythmic interest:

Fig. 2-5

Here is another example that mixes both 5/8 and 3/8 phrases against 4/4:

Fig. 2-6

When you hear jazz players playing long lines that nevertheless sustain interest, it is likely they are using the polyrhythms shown in previous examples or others similar to them.

Harmonic Dislocation

Another device also used to create rhythmic tension and interest is a technique I call harmonic dislocation. Take this common "Rhythm changes" phrase as an example:

Fig. 2-7

By playing the phrase one beat later we get:

Fig. 2-8

Here is another typical phrase over the same section that uses an eighth pick-up to the downbeat:

Fig. 2-9

Shifting over one beat, we get:

Fig. 2-10

This tension is caused by harmonic dislocation. Another good way to demonstrate this is by playing chords displaced in the same manner.

CHAPTER 2 REFINING / ENHANCING LINES WITH RHYTHMIC DEVICES

These are the chord changes of the original:

Fig. 2-11

Same changes shifted over one beat:

Fig. 2-12

In Fig. 2-9 this is the harmonic progression:

Fig. 2-13

Moved over one beat:

Fig. 2-14

I will now write a solo using some of the devices discussed thus far. I will use the chords to Van Heusen's "Here's That Rainy Day." This tune starts out like the first chord changes used (chord variation A). Below is an analysis of some of the key phrases of the solo.

Fig. 2-15 Jimmy Raney solo on changes to "Here's That Rainy Day" (first 16 bars):

Solo Analysis

In the first two bars I use the 3/8 groupings against 4/8 which creates built in syncopations:

In bar 3 we have upbeat quarters (more syncopation). Also note the flatted 5th in bars 2 and 3, which nevertheless sound melodic because they are notes in the key (F) scale:

Fig. 2-16

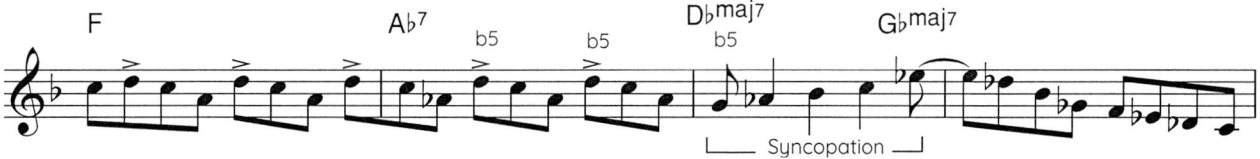

In bar 10 there is dislocated harmony. The straight (or perhaps expected) way to play this phrase would be:

Fig. 2-17

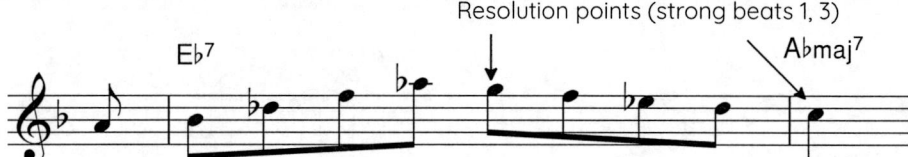

Played this way, the 7th (A♭) of B♭-7 resolves to the third (G) of the E♭7 on beat 3 and the 3rd of A♭ (C) comes right on beat one. These are the strong beats of the bar. However, in the solo, with one beat later displacement, the 7-3 resolutions occur on the 4th and 2nd beats of the bar respectively. Two and four are weak beats so you have delayed resolutions, giving tension (see Fig. 2-18).

Fig. 2-18

The effect of the displacement can be heard clearly by playing chords. Instead of this:

Fig. 2-19

You get this:

Fig. 2-20

THINGS TO THINK ABOUT

- Mixing 3/8 and 5/8 accented scale patterns with 2/4 and 4/4 are very useful for creating more interest on a continuous line.
    - Use scale and arpeggio sequences as a "quick and dirty" way to create polyrhythms (see Figs. 2-5, 2-6, 2-15).
- Learn whichever phrases you know on different beats. Experiment by starting on every eighth note subdivision within a measure. (Figs. 2-17, 2-18)
- Make sure you know how to get back to beat 1 when you do odd meter tricks. (Fig. 2-16)
- Don't overdo rhythmic devices. Use them to enhance your existing "straight" lines.

CHAPTER 3: SEQUENCE & DEVELOPMENT OF LINE

Sequence adds direction and interest to melodic line, especially when they are used with subtle variations, both harmonic and rhythmic. Quotes Jimmy:

"There is a lot of sequential stuff in my playing that's hidden sometimes . . . in other words there will be sequences . . . but they're decorated or hidden. . . . The structure of your playing comes from cohesion from sequences and patterns, but you can't make them too obvious."

Fig. 3-1 features a great sequence from bar 26 of his play-along track, on "Nowhere" which repeats the first 6 notes of the first half, then rises a third above the original, makes a harmonic alteration a m3 above (to fit the minor IV chord) and continues the imitation. Note how the second half makes the entire phrase more climactic and with feeling for partial cadence.

Fig. 3-1[1]

Frequently sequential and polyrhythmic devices are used together to build phrases.

This is a sequence implying 5/4 polyrhythm against 4/4 rhythm. Do you feel the tension created?

Fig. 3-2

If it were 4/4 against 4/4 there would be no tension:

Fig. 3-3

The 5/4 phrase could be done three times, finally resolving back to straight 4/4 on the A minor chord:

Fig. 3-4

---
1. Jimmy Raney, *Play Along with Jimmy Raney, Vol. 20*, Jamey Aebersold Jazz, 1979

The below solo sample in Fig. 3-5 in bars 7-8 over the changes to *Out of Nowhere* uses the "hiding the sequence" technique quoted at the top of the chapter. It is an asymmetrical sequence. The first F7 phrase implies 3/4 but the second E7 phrase—although imitative—is longer in length and uses different 9ths (F9 vs. E7♯9) although they are on the same notes (E, F):

Fig. 3-5[2]

Although initiating a 3/4 over 4/4 feel, this phrase seems more indicative of 3 + 5 asymmetric 8/8 division. For example, the Fig. 3-5 phrase re-beamed below seems to be most in sync conceptually while counting, "1, 2, 3   1, 2, 3, 4, 5   1, 2, 3. . ." (See Fig. 3-6).

Fig. 3-6

Fig. 3-7 shows another asymmetrical polyrhythmic sequence bars 1-4 of his 3rd chorus of Jimmy's solo to "How About You" from *Live in Tokyo*. It also begins with 3/4 pentatonic phrases then elongates to 4/4 to meet the next downbeat. The implied harmony is shown but essentially the line is moving from E♭ major to E major tonalities.

Fig. 3-7[3]

"A good line starts with an idea and builds from there, often using sequences-repeating the idea starting on a different note and during a different chord. Maybe also starting on a different beat. Perhaps even an upbeat."

Jimmy's above quote is reflected in the line played during a recorded lesson in Fig. 3-8. The phrase uses a subtle sequence by displacing the second imitation. Note how the 7-3 enclosure (A-F♯-G-G♯) starts on beat 1 of the E7 chord but the related enclosure starts on the upbeat to beat 1 of D7 chord enclosure (G-E-F-F♯).

---

2. Ibid.
3. Jimmy Raney, *Live in Tokyo,* Xanadu, 1976

CHAPTER 3 SEQUENCE & DEVELOPMENT OF LINE

Fig. 3-8

Analyzing further, there is implied polymeter with two 6/4 phrases, with additional sub accents in 3/8 which resolve to the 3rd of G on beat 1, bar 4. (See analysis below.) This attests to Jimmy's mastery in reconciling metrical space instinctively, after having introduced displacement and asymmetry prior.

Fig. 3-9

Fig. 3-10 is an example of asymmetrical development that begins with a 3/8 pattern, germinates a second 2 count sequential nugget ("12, 12") on the latter half of its ending, and is developed further. To better illustrate the sequence, verbalized eighth note counts are shown with the passage.

Fig. 3-10[4]

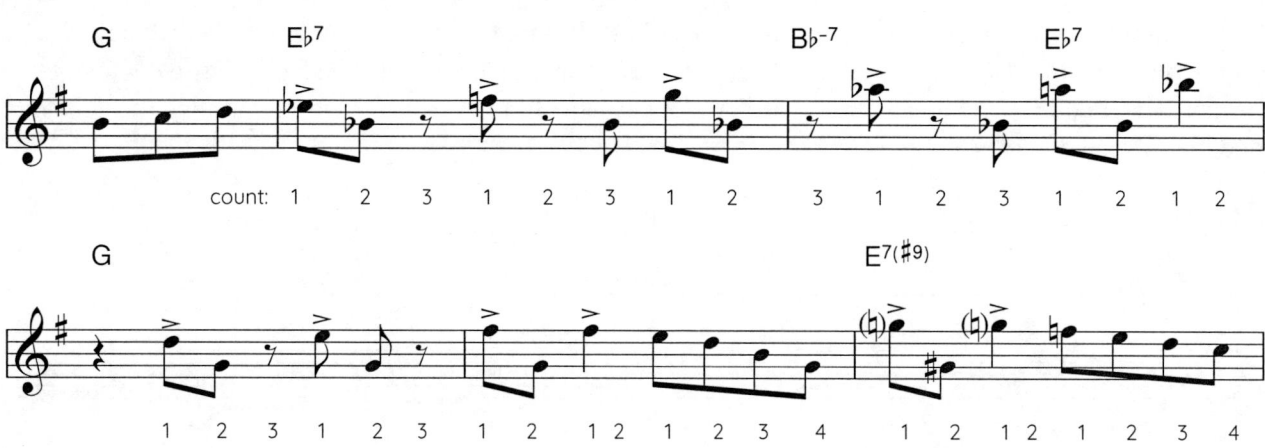

Note how the second 3/8 (count: "123") pattern repeats only twice the second time and starts on beat 2, meeting the downbeat of bar 22. Also note how a new theme and answer of 12 12 1234 is developed in measures 22 and 23 based on the "1 2" rhythm and 7th interval of measure 20.

---

4. Raney, *Play Along Vol. 20.*

THINGS TO THINK ABOUT

- Generally, avoid using exact or obvious repetition for sequence. (Figs. 3-3, 3-4)
- For variety, continue sequences on different beats. (Fig. 3-9)
- Try using sequence over sections that change in harmony for more interesting results. (Fig. 3-6)
- Different parts of the original motive may be also used as sequence material. (Fig. 3-10)
- Combine sequence with rhythmic devices, such as polymeter. (Fig. 3-7)

CHAPTER 4: INTERVALLIC AND DIRECTIONAL VARIETY IN LINE

A common fault of inexperienced players is using too many consecutive scale notes without varying the intervals or linear direction. It's important to make sure your improvised line is a balanced mixture of intervals, scales, thirds (broken chords), chromatics and skips (intervals of a fourth or larger).

You want to avoid too many scale passages such as:

Fig 4-1

Changing direction sooner helps:

Fig 4-2

Adding altered notes and changes of directions:

Fig 4-3

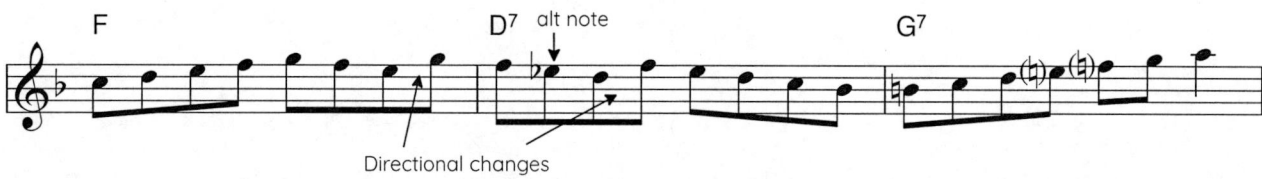

Fig 4-4

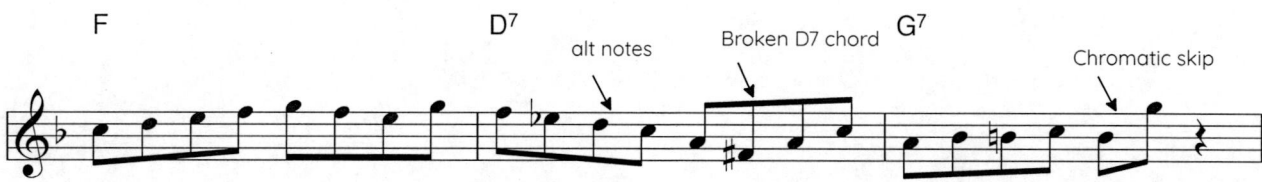

Now we are getting an interesting line. It has scales with changes in direction, altered tones (suspensions) #9 and ♭9 on the D7 chord, a broken D7 chord, chromatics, and a leap (skip) of a minor 6th. Note that we are still playing straight 8th notes with no pause in between.

By comparing Fig 4-4 with Fig 4-1, you can easily see how much more interesting 4-4 is than 4-1. Let us try building a solo from this phrase:

Fig 4-5

Now we have repeated the phrase exactly except for the downward motion of the skip. We can vastly improve it thus:

Fig 4-6

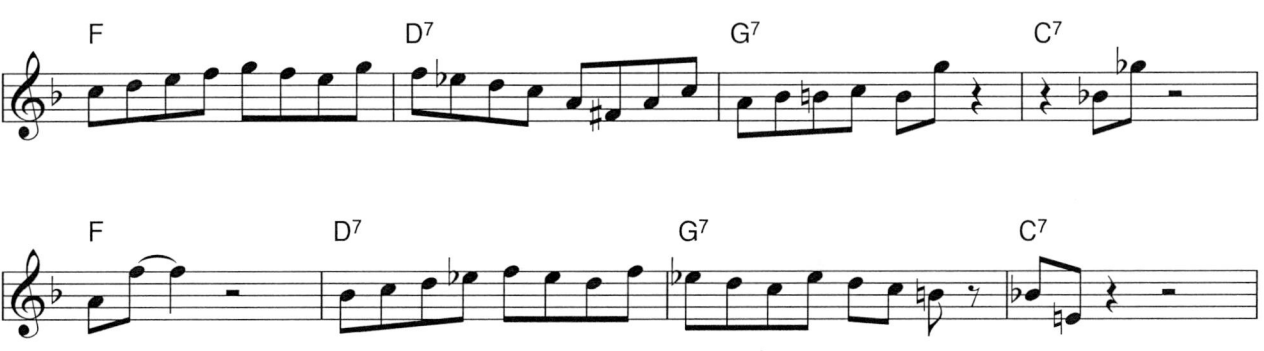

Now we still have the sequence, but we have played the skip three times. Notice that it repeats every 3 beats giving a 3/4 against 4/4 grouping.

Fig. 4-7

CHAPTER 4 INTERVALLIC AND DIRECTIONAL VARIETY IN LINE

Note also we have a 5-bar phrase before the sequence begins again starting this time on the D7 chord:

Fig. 4-8

The sequence is now one step lower giving augmented fifth, raised and flatted ninths (part of an E♭ scale against a D7 chord). So, we now have a 5-bar phrase followed by a 3-bar phrase (asymmetry), implied 3/4 meter against 4/4 more altered notes.

Although it is generally more acceptable to play more consecutive scale notes as tempos increase (to cover more ground), it is still more effective to vary the line direction at up tempos, because it is more creative and thoughtful approach. For example, at 250 bpm, the line in Fig. 4-9 would be a plausible jazz line over the progression:

Fig. 4-9

But it falls flat in comparison to line in Fig. 4-10 which breaks up the line direction and features more rhythmic, melodic, and harmonic interest:

Fig. 4-10

THINGS TO THINK ABOUT

- Weave lines with more changes of direction. (Fig. 4-3)
- Avoid continuous uniform motion of scales up or down.*(Fig. 4-1)
- Intersperse skips and broken chords with scales for variety. (Fig. 4-4)
- Create rhythmic interest in long scalar lines by grouping measures asymmetrically. (Fig. 4-8)

*Note:

On faster tempos, long passages of consecutive scale notes may be more acceptable and common given there are generally more notes per change. However, it also true that master beboppers (like Jimmy and Barry Harris for example) will change directions in line even at up-tempos, projecting the feeling of "thinking faster" than the rest of us.

SECTION II

- BACKGROUND/HISTORY
- CONCEPTS IN RECORDINGS

CHAPTER 5: JIMMY RANEY'S POLYRHYTHMIC DEVICES IN RECORDINGS

Background/History

Although much is justifiably made of Jimmy's melodic genius, Jimmy's innovations regarding *rhythmic conception* are perhaps overlooked and underemphasized. Polymeter is at the heart of Jimmy's broader conception and approach to playing over changes. Many of these concepts can be traced back to his earliest influences. Charlie Parker's *Savoy* recordings were hugely influential on Jimmy, who mastered many instrumental solos from the Parker recordings note for note. Friend and colleague, Stan Getz also had an impact on Jimmy's playing, and they picked up many things from each other by osmosis on the bandstand. Both Stan and Jimmy went on to develop their own personal styles built originally from the Parker and Lester Young models.

Charlie Parker's influence

This famous arpeggio phrase by Parker from the 2nd chorus bridge of the legendary "Koko" solo is deceptively complex. It's actually an implied 7/4 phrase (3+2+2). This solo was easily the most famous bebop solo of its time. More on Parker's influence will be discussed later.

Fig. 5-1[5]

Stan Getz's influence

On the classic *Live at Storyville* sessions, Getz frequently used Parker influenced polyrhythmic scales and arpeggios over fast tunes. These types of devices were already somewhat present in Jimmy's playing (see Figs. 5-8, 5-9), but not quite as forcefully yet as was the case with Getz at that point (1949-1951) especially on up-tempo numbers. Below are 6/8 patterns from his solo to "Mosquito Knees" in bars 26-30 and in the 4th chorus, bars 1-4 (in Fig. 5-3):

Fig. 5-2[6]

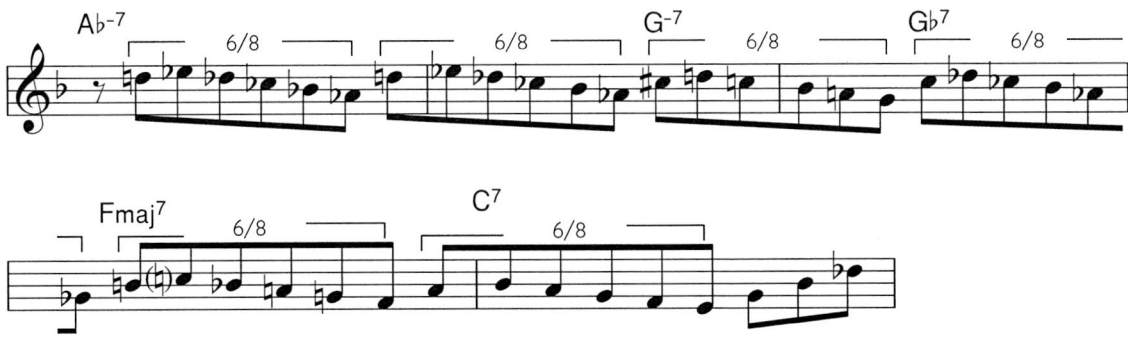

---

5. Charlie Parker, *The Savoy Recordings,* Savoy, 1945
6. Stan Getz, Jazz at Storyville — The Stan Getz Quintet, Roost, 1951

Fig. 5-3[7]

Polyrhythmic scale patterns

This is a "Raney style" 5/8 scale pattern (like an early lesson I heard demonstrated to Doug) used on one of Jimmy's favorite solo vehicles, "Just Friends." Notice the mode changes to fit the chords:

Fig. 5-4

Here's another of Jimmy's favorite scale fragment patterns in 6/8 used typically on the changes of bars 15-16 of "Just Friends."

Fig. 5-5

Also note the contrast in motion between the upward scales (C- C#- D-) and the downward harmony (C-7 B7 B♭).

Fig. 5-6 shows a 6/8 scalar polyrhythm Jimmy started in his 6th chorus over the transition to the IV chord in Parker's "Billie's Bounce" and continues to bar 9, from a live gig in 1984:

---

7. Ibid.

Fig. 5-6[8]

Note how the 6/8 pattern is broken briefly in the 3rd measure to get back on track to the A-7 in the 4th measure, and how the Ab- pattern is deftly transitioned mid-bar to the G-7 chord. Jimmy was always keenly aware of his place in the music no matter what rhythmic devices he employed.

Fig. 5-7 is a similar scale pattern Jimmy played over the changes to "Out of Nowhere." Note how the scale pattern modulates down a half step and then up a flatted 5th:

Fig. 5-7[9]

Polyrhythmic arpeggio patterns

When playing polyrhythmic arpeggios, Jimmy typically plays 3/4-meter sweeps on 7th arpeggios against 4/4. He also usually makes melodic adjustments to fit changes in the harmony. Below is a polyrhythmic phrase Jimmy played on his own composition, "Parker 51" 2nd solo chorus, bars 4-6:

Fig. 5-8[10]

---

8. Jimmy Raney, *Jimmy Raney in Nashville*, Private Video Collection, 1984
9. Raney, *Play Along, Vol. 20*
10. Getz, *Storyville*

CHAPTER 5 JIMMY RANEY'S POLYRHYTHMIC DEVICES IN RECORDINGS

A similar arpeggio phrase follows on the 1st bar of the bridge of the same solo chorus:

Fig. 5-9[11]

As shown in previous two examples, his early polyrhythmic efforts were more conservative in terms of rhythmic placement, starting on beat 1. Later, he would open things up a bit more, for example in this 1954 recording of his solo to "Cherokee," he starts the 3/4 pattern on beat 2:

Fig. 5-10[12]

In this arpeggio line Jimmy played on Vol 20 play-along instruction book over "Friends," the phrase outlines the 3rd to 9th arpeggios in a progression from B♭maj to B♭- but starts in the middle of the bar.

Fig. 5-11[13]

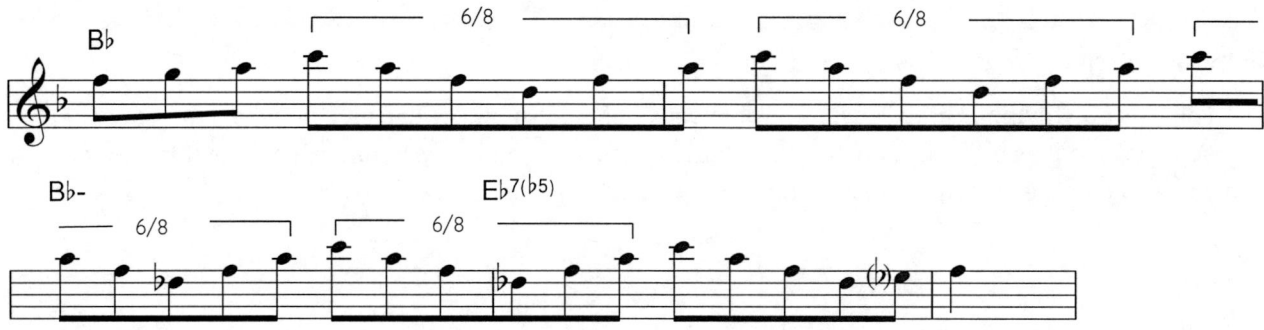

It is important to note in three of these examples that the harmony can be displaced from one: anticipating (Fig. 5-10) or delaying (Fig. 5-9 & 5-11) to suit the line. This demonstrates the interconnected nature of displacement and polyrhythm in Raney's style. Polyrhythmic approaches are ideally suited for Jimmy's concept of freeing improvised line from the bar line because they are periodic, un-grounding and then re-grounding by design.

---

11. Ibid.
12. Jimmy Raney, *Jimmy Raney Visits Paris, Vol. 2, Vogue,* 1954
13. Raney, *Play Along, Vol. 20*

On a videotaped gig in 1987 with Cal Collins, Jimmy played a similar arpeggio sequence over "Just Friends" as Fig. 5-11, but he initiated the line with a pickup on the "and" of 3 in Fig. 5-12. The line continues to anticipate 1 as the chord anticipates the B♭- chord:

Fig. 5-12[14]

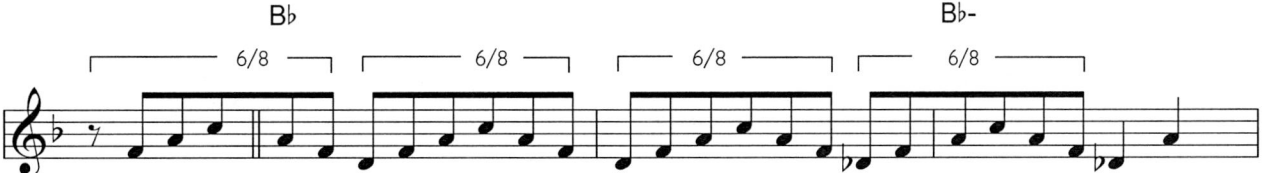

Polyrhythmic general phrase patterns

In addition to polyrhythmic scale and arpeggio patterns, Jimmy also uses short lick and rhythmic phrase patterns to break up the time. Fig. 5-13 and 5-14 shows some good examples of this on a solo to his own composition, "Momentum," bars 2-3, and a few years earlier on "Stella by Starlight," bars 7-8:

Fig. 5-13[15]

Fig. 5-14[16]

Here's a similar pattern on his 2nd solo chorus to his tune, "Motion" in Fig. 5-15, bars 1-4. Note the mixed eighth-quarter combinations, the 5th ostinato on "A" and "B♭" and the rise and fall of the upper notes against them. This combination of factors makes the entire passage feel like two 6/4 phrases. Seemingly simple, these techniques reflect Jimmy's rhythmic improvisational skill and his knack for creating subtle sequences.

---

14. Jimmy Raney/Cal Collins, *Live at the Actors Theatre, Louisville,* Private Video Collection, 1987
15. Jimmy Raney, *Momentum,* MPS, 1974
16. Jimmy Raney, *Strings and Swings,* Muse, 1969

Fig. 5-15[17]

Fig. 5-16 shows short 3/4 chord resolution patterns used on his composition, "Signal" to navigate a 2-bar turnaround, (bars 13-15) each note group executed with a rest and a pickup:

Fig. 5-16[18]

Polyrhythmic blues lick patterns

Jimmy often does bluesy finger slur licks in 3/8 patterns. In standards, this often involves transposing with the change; here are examples on "Momentum," bars 27-29, 1st chorus and bars 3-5, 2nd chorus:

Fig. 5-17[19]

Fig. 5-18[20]

Sometimes he adds thirds or chord fragments to the 3/8 Figures to make them more interesting as in Fig. 5-19 during drums trades on "Anthropology," and Fig 5-20 on "Stella by Starlight," bars 17-19 (3rd chorus):

---

17. Jimmy Raney, *Play Duets with Jimmy Raney, Vol. 29,* Jamey Aebersold Jazz, 1983
18. Jimmy Raney, *Jimmy Raney Plays,* Prestige, 1953
19. Raney, *Momentum*
20. Ibid.

Fig. 5-19[21]

Fig. 5-20[22]

One of Jimmy's most recognizable licks is the one he uses in Fig. 5-21. He uses it blues and standards, and generally in 3/4 polyrhythm, though occasionally others. See bars 6-8, "Blues for Wes":

Fig. 5-21[23]

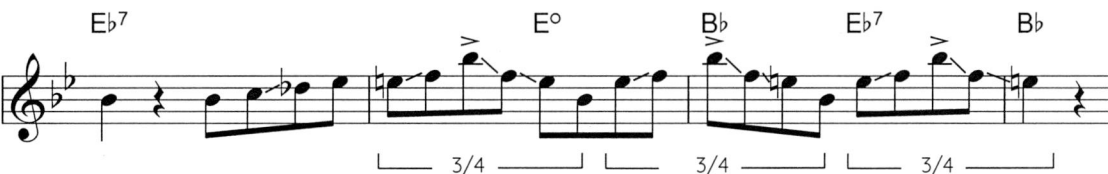

When Jimmy is using this blues phrase in a standards context, it often involves transposing the phrase sequentially to fit the chords. See Fig. 5-22 over "What is This Thing Called Love," bars 15-20, 3rd chorus:

Fig. 5-22[24]

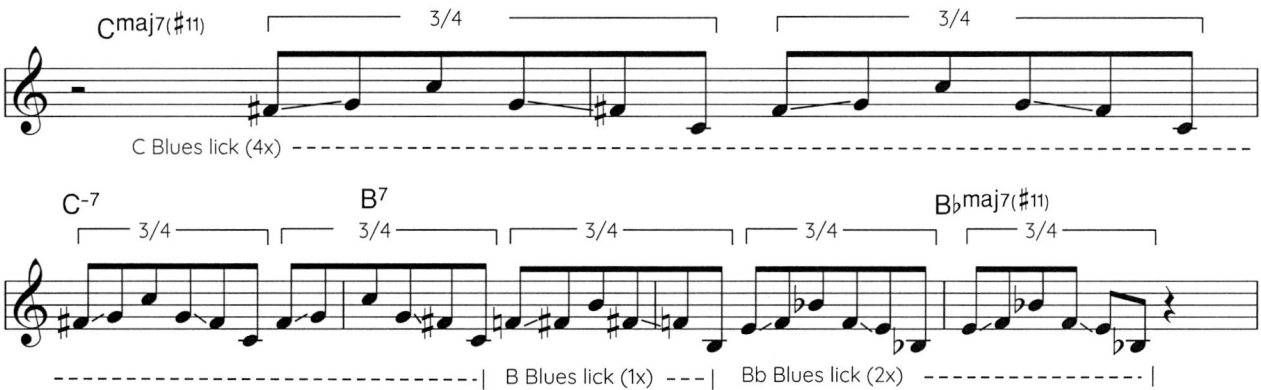

---

21. Raney, Live in Tokyo
22. Raney, Strings & Swings
23. Raney, Play Along, Vol. 20
24. Jimmy Raney, Raney '81, Criss Cross, 1981

Note how the blues licks phrase starts two bars before the bridge, descends from C to B to B♭ with the harmony and finishes comfortably on the downbeat of the B♭ chord for the last iteration of the lick.

Jimmy sometimes pauses between iterations of this ♭5 lick, which leads to interesting metrical implications. In Fig. 5-23 in his first solo chorus to "Anthropology" (bars 26-28), the phrase implies a 6/4 because the lick starts on the 2nd beat of the bar and the repeat starts on 4th beat of the next measure. It is important to perceive each phrase from attack point to attack point so that silence is also part of the count.

Fig. 5-23[25]

In Fig. 5-24 on the drum trade fours before the last head on Hod O'Brien's "Instant Blue," Jimmy uses the blues lick similar to the previous example but in 5/4 rhythm. Again, it is important to view rests as part of the count.

Fig. 5-24[26]

---

25. Raney, *Live in Tokyo*
26. Ted Brown, *In Good Company,* Criss Cross, 1985

THINGS TO THINK ABOUT

- When Jimmy created polyrhythmic licks, he also:
    - Used rhythmic variations of the construction. (See Figs. 5-23, 5-24)
    - Transposed them sequentially thru changes (Fig. 5-22)
- When playing polyrhythmically, he thought carefully and when necessary, planned about how he wanted to resolve the rhythm. (Figs. 5-4, 5-17)
- Juxtaposed polyrhythmic blues licks into a standards context for interesting results. (Fig. 5-18)
- Always practiced polyrhythms and worked them out in the context of tunes so that they were not mechanical. (Figs. 5-20, 5-22)
- Rhythm adds dimension and weight to improvised line; Jimmy's frequent use of it suggests thinking about the rhythmic implications of improvisations before the melodic ones.

CHAPTER 6: JIMMY RANEY'S DISPLACEMENT CONCEPTS IN RECORDINGS

Harmonic Dislocation

In a widely circulated guitar lesson, Jimmy described his phrasing approach as a kind of weaving displacement process of tension and release, like the dissonance/consonance concept in harmony. He achieves this by starting phrases earlier or later than expected, then adding or subtracting notes to bring them back into the time. This tension and displacement create bar line transcendence. Jimmy's displacement and polymetric concepts are intertwined. Unusual start places can be reconciled by polymeter concepts which reground the phrasing in predictable measures.

Fig. 6-1 shows a sample of this technique on the 3rd chorus of his solo to "I Could Write a Book," bars 19-22. In addition to this standard bebop phrase starting a beat later than is typical (on 2+ rather than 1+), the displacement continues because of the consistent emphasis on weak beats 2 and 4. (See notations in excerpt). It comes back to the strong beat in the beginning of the 4th measure.

Fig. 6-1[27]

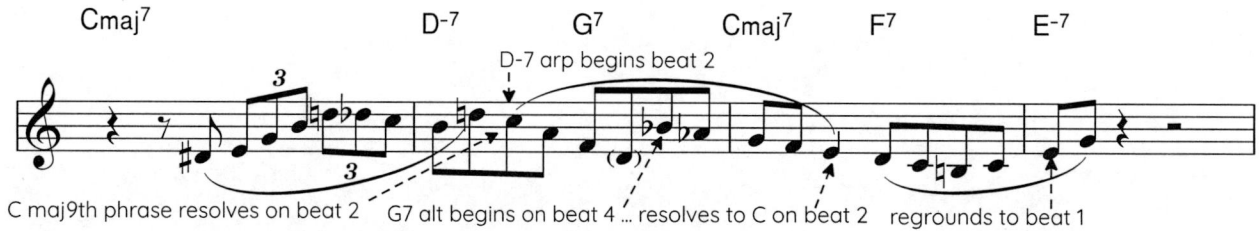

To demonstrate further, Fig. 6-2 shows the same phrase put in its more "likely" place on the "and" of one. It is more stable with the harmonic resolution points now on strong beats 1 and 3, however the interest from weak beat tension is no longer there, as was previously discussed in Chapter 2 (Fig. 2-18). Jimmy is clearly modeling the concepts he learned from his idol, Charlie Parker, who used the same rhythmic flexibility in his patented phrases.

Fig. 6-2

A similar Parker type displaced phrase occurs in his "Anthropology" solo from *Live in Tokyo* (2nd chorus, solo bars 26-30), but uses anticipated placement rather than delayed — putting much of the strong accents on the 2nd and 4th beats until the phrase "rights itself" by arriving on the 3rd of C7 on the downbeat of the next measure, essentially dividing the 2-measure unit unevenly into 5+3.

---

27. Jimmy Raney, *Wistaria*, Criss Cross, 1985

Fig. 6-3[28]

Fig. 6-4 shows the same phrase realized with the more common placement of the triplet arpeggio phrase on the "and" of 1. The solution would be initially more "rhythmically comfortable" with the D – F triplet slur on beat 3 and the D-7 G7♭9 enclosure the next bar on beats 1 to 3; however, this would defeat the 7-3 resolution and beat reconciliation on C7 referred to previously.

Fig. 6-4

Fig. 6-5 shows another phrase from the beginning of the "Anthropology" solo. It throws you because you are expecting this type of phrase to begin on beat 1. However, in hindsight, its use on beat 2 is perfect because the phrase then resolves rhythmically on the 1st beat of the next bar targeting the 3rd of F7.

Fig. 6-5[29]

There is a distinct feeling of 3 when listening carefully to this phrase. (This will be discussed later in Section III). This is reinforced by the C♯-7 phrase which begins after 3 beats. I have alternatively beamed the excerpt in Fig. 6-6 to show this. In essence, the entire phrase can be seen as a multi-measure syncopation in 3/4 with the 1st beat displacement completed with the final 2 beat phrase (i.e., 1 | 123 | 123 | 123 | 12).

Fig. 6-6

---

28. Raney, *Live in Tokyo*
29. Ibid.

CHAPTER 6 JIMMY RANEY'S DISPLACEMENT CONCEPTS IN RECORDINGS

Add/Subtract concepts

The technique of dislocation requires understanding the metric effect of the displacement and how exactly to offset that. One of Jimmy Raney's techniques for doing this is by addition/subtraction and he has talked about this specifically in lessons. Again, the displacement/relocation technique in Jimmy's style usually involves playing larger meters over the bar line. But the technique is usually a semi-conscious process.

Fig. 6-7 is an example of the rhythmic "add/subtract" soloing concept, over the changes to "How About You," bars 9-12:

Fig. 6-7[30]

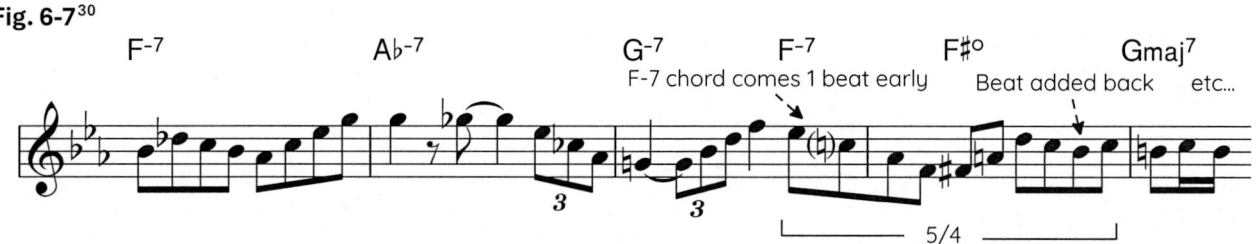

and bars 28-32 same solo:

Fig. 6-8

Below is an across the bar line appraisal with displacement analysis of the same passage:

Fig. 6-9

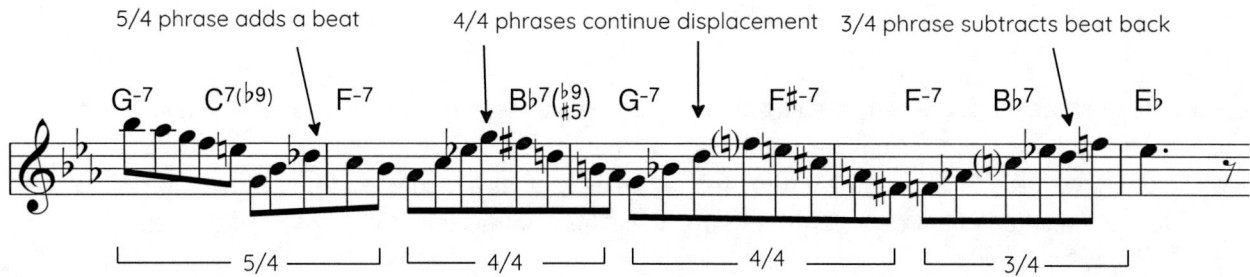

As mentioned earlier and as evidenced by these analyses, Jimmy's displacement is interwoven with polymeter, achieving rhythmic tension against the meter, and then resolving to strong beats by rhythmically astute adjustment. More advanced examples of these concepts in Raney solos are explored in the next chapter.

---

30. Raney, *Play Along, Vol. 20*

THE JIMMY RANEY BOOK

Free (unresolved) displacement

The last solo example over Bob Brookmeyer's "Passport to Pimlico," bars 29-33, shows Jimmy just embracing the tension created by moving to an obviously displaced beat. Fig. 6-10 is perhaps the most overt Raney example of this, faking everyone out by seemingly turning the beat around for several measures until finally hitting the D♭ tonic on the downbeat. That is the kind of trickery Parker pulled on his rhythm sections!

Fig. 6-10[31]

It may not be clear from the notation what is going on here (other than the start on beat 2). Fig. 6-11 is what the phrasing of the previous example really "feels like" as played by Jimmy:

Fig. 6-11 (Fig. 6-10 re-beamed)

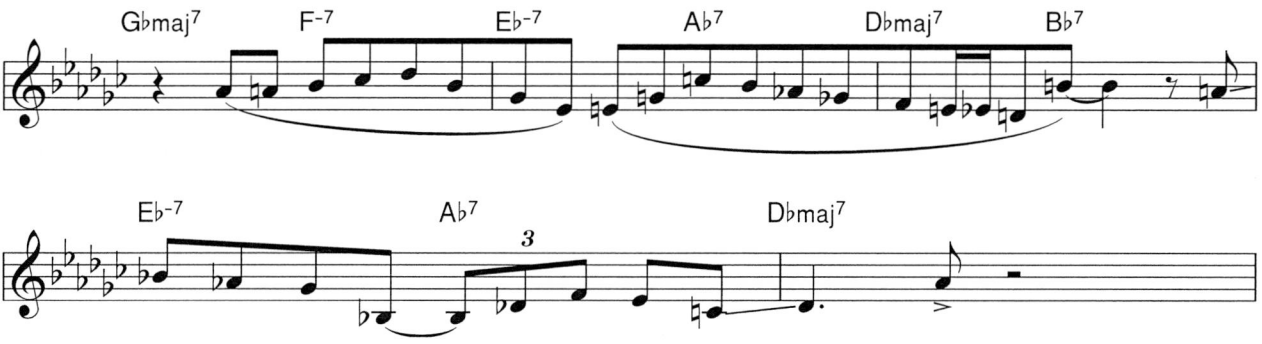

Fig. 6-12 is a clearer case of harmonic displacement, but it is a more extreme case, where the implied harmony (shown underneath) over "There Will Never Be Another You" (2nd chorus, bars 5-12) is roughly a measure late throughout for the sake of tension until it hits the tonic chord.

---

31. Jimmy Raney, *In Three Attitudes,* ABC Paramount,

Fig. 6-12[32]

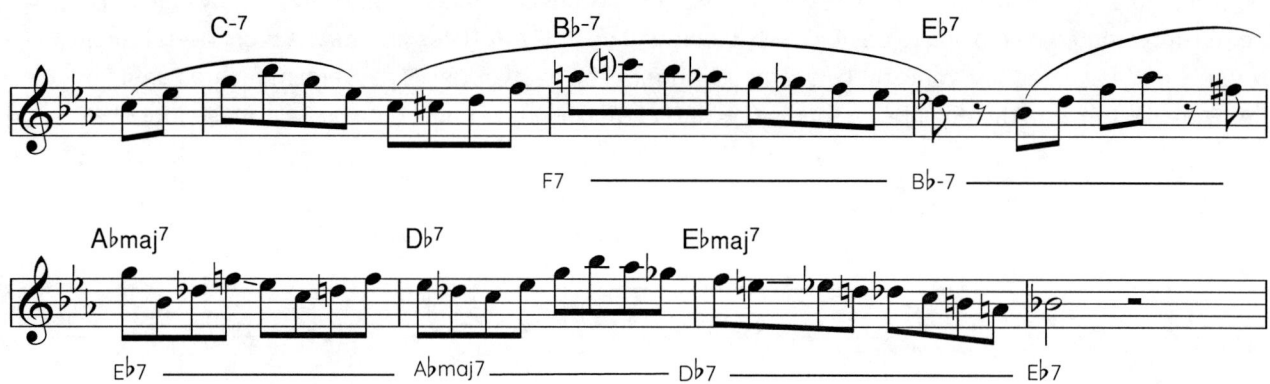

---

32. Jimmy Raney, *The Influence,* Xanadu, 1975

THINGS TO THINK ABOUT

- Harmonic Dislocation:
  - Jimmy takes typical phrases played on beat 1 or the "and" of one and moves them to unexpected places to create rhythmic interest and tension. (Figs. 6-2, 6-3)
- Add/Subtract Technique:
  - Beat adding involves extending across the bar line, then reconciling it with a shorter follow-up phrase and connecting to the first beat of the next bar. (See Fig. 6-9)
  - Beat subtracting involves anticipating the bar line early, then reconciling by adding additional notes to connect to the first beat of the next bar. (See Fig. 6-7)
  - To demonstrate further, see below example utilizing both techniques:

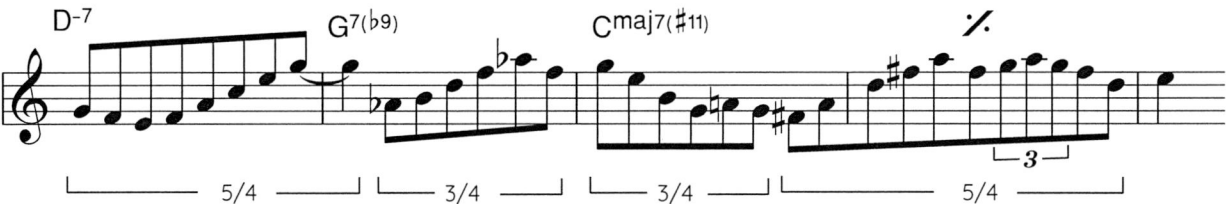

- Seeing how 3/4 phrases resolve on different beats and learning how they "feel" thru repetition establishes comfort with polymeter. (See Fig. 6-5 and also the later section "Undercurrent of Three")
- When using dislocation techniques, strong harmony notes like the 3rd are important resolution "anchors" (Figs. 6-3, 6-5).

CHAPTER 7: JIMMY RANEY'S ADVANCED ASYMMETRY & POLYMETRICS IN RECORDINGS

There is little to conclusively suggest that the terms polyrhythm and polymeter are not interchangeable. However, to describe the nuances of Jimmy's rhythmic devices, it is necessary to differentiate the two. For analysis purposes, polyrhythm refers to a specific scale, arpeggio or phrase nugget **repeated intentionally in rhythm;** polymeter refers to phrasing, grouping, and/or accenting notes across the bar line, implying a **larger metric space.** Polymeter often also necessitates analysis of silence and phrase arcs (the bottoms and tops of phrases, how they are accented, executed etc.).

Jimmy mastered both polyrhythmic and polymetric conceptions, but more in an unconscious or semi-conscious manner. Jimmy has said himself, "It's almost easier to do it, than explain it." The complexity of his own playing could even escape his own analysis because of the ex post facto nature of that appraisal. For example, Fig. 7-1 shows a II-IVm polyrhythmic scale pattern he demonstrated in a guitar lesson, describing it as "6 and 6 or something . . . " (Two 6/4 phrases) The example is in fact two 7/4 phrases!

Concepts in Practice

Fig. 7-1

For those of you sticklers, you'll note the first phrase is in fact, 13 eighth notes, not 14 as in the second one. I would resist interpreting this as the more complex 13/8 + 7/4, however. Generally, Jimmy played his ascending scale patterns with a lower neighbor tone as in the second B♭- phrase (on "A") He simply just started on the downbeat. As further defense, check out the similar solo scale pattern played on "Just Friends" from the 1987 Actor's Theatre gig in Louisville (with Cal Collins) in Fig. 7-2. The phrases are all with lower neighbors and 7/4 exactly.

Fig. 7-2[33]

Another stunning feature of the Fig. 7-2 solo segment is where it starts, the "and" of 3. But the 3+ start makes total sense as the third 7/4 phrase ending coincides with the G-7 bar beginning the last 8 bars of the form. Stated another way, he was intuitively aware of the metric space of 6 bars he was dealing with when he started the pattern: 7/4 x 3=21 beats plus 3 total beats of silence. He would in fact have been perfectly re-grounded to beat 1 had he chosen to do a 4th iteration of the sequence in G- with a pick-up eighth on F♯.

---

33. Raney/Collins, *Actors Theatre*

Figure 7-3 shows an instance where Jimmy IS playing a 6+6 polyrhythm over "Anthropology." It is a long pentatonic phrase sequence that moves up a m3 on the second iteration on his 4th solo chorus, bars 2-7. It is most natural when counting it, "123456, 12-12-12," with the latter half like a hemiola in duple meter:

Fig. 7-3[34]

Parker's influence on Jimmy Raney's dislocation/polymetric concept

It is often noted that Jimmy's mastery of the subtler rhythmic aspects of Parker's language is what sets him apart as one of the most significant interpreters of bebop on the guitar. His penchant for rhythmic asymmetry was a direct Charlie Parker influence and particularly from certain solos, notably (by his own admission to me) "Koko" and in the instrumental solo out-choruses. The solo's continuous string of eighth notes, cross bar line phrasing and accents, and weaving mid-bar resolutions is a crucial influence on these same Raney concepts discussed in this book.

Rearranging the solo according to its strong phrase lengths (direction, arpeggio implications, accents, etc.) my interpretation of the solo's phrase polymetric grouping is 5+5+6 x2. There are some who may regard this as speculative. I would venture that if you learned how to play this phrase, you would key in on the important 1st harmonic segments (the G-7, F#o, G7♭9) how it resolves to the 3rd of C7 and fall into the very rhythms I described. Likewise, the strong D-7 C#-7 phrase that implies 5/4 beginning in bar 5.

Fig. 7-4[35]

The advanced rhythmic complexity of Parker's "continuous line" passage undoubtedly made a major impression on Jimmy, especially in his approach playing fast tunes and "Rhythm Changes." There are several examples of this influence on the Live in Tokyo record. For example, on his quicksilver version of "Stella by Starlight" he plays many complicated and risky rhythmic phrases and does it without rhythm section support or obvious timekeeping.

---

34. Raney, *Live in Tokyo*
35. Charlie Parker, *The Savoy Recordings,* Savoy, 1945

The first line where this type of asymmetrical grouping sticks out is the passage in Fig. 7-5 in bars 1-9. Much is my interpretation of the grouping, but this is what I think is going on in his 3rd chorus:

The first **six beat G major phrase** is immediately followed by **C#-7 phrase** that cuts in **2 beats ahead of the bar** (I interpret the D and C♮ notes as chromatic neighbor tones to C#). **The C7 phrase continues that 2-beat anticipation** (aka subtraction) and this continues until it is **corrected** by the **next two 5/4 groupings** which *add back 2 beats.* By the time **the note D** of the D-7 chord is played, he is **reconciled to beat 1** (in 7th bar of passage), and two exact II-V phrases are repeated an 8ve apart to finish the 8 bars:

Fig. 7-5[36]

At the top of the 4th chorus, he again plays a complex phrase dividing 8 measures creatively as in Parker's example. Again, the rhythmic interpretation might be subjective, but here is some of my reasoning:

The **first phrase** is a clear **C#-7 F#7** (the G natural is a mis-hit and intended note was probably an E). The **next phrase** is Jimmy's characteristic **cross-cutting multiple neighbor tone to G** (A-G-E♭-F-A). Normally, I would say that the G tonality is reconciled to the downbeat of the 3rd measure, but Jimmy **clearly plays thru the next phrase** (where the B becomes a N.T. of C) **with the next strong phrase on the A-11 arpeggio,** which is then combined with a **strong D-G7 phrase.** Then there are **strong 3/4 arpeggios on G7♭9, C major and C minor** to end the phrase.

---

36. Raney, *Live in Tokyo*

Fig. 7-6[37]

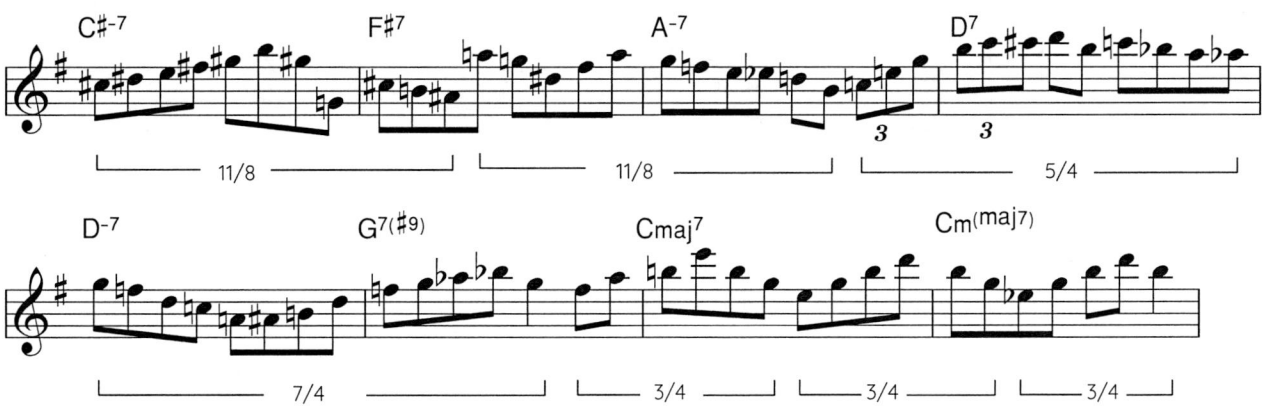

It is important to point out that this rhythmic interpretation has more to do with an appraisal how Jimmy constructs his phrases on an *intuitive level*. I do not believe he plans how he divides the space; he does this in a manner of feeling an asymmetrical tension, pursuing it but always knowing how it resolves. The same way you would approach choosing a chord color in an accompaniment, it just *feels like* the right amount of "harmonic spice" to the moment. In this case a "rhythmic spice" and this is consistent with the statements Jimmy made about it in the beginning of Chapter 6.

The beginning of the "Anthropology" solo from *Live in Tokyo* demonstrates a more space oriented complex meter approach. Jimmy starts the solo much more in a "blues mode" than his customary change-oriented style. He plays three phrases and the most fundamental way to see them is an astonishing 3 x11=33, traversing the first 8 bars with an extra beat and starting the next phrase with displacement.

Fig. 7-7[38]

Another signature sound of Jimmy's is his "wide arpeggio" sweeps he developed in the '60's. It certainly reflects his absorption into classical music and the cello. The excerpt in Fig. 7-8 shows a 7+9 beat grouping of 4 measures using these sweeps over "Stella by Starlight," bars 19-24, 3rd solo chorus:

---

37. Raney, *Live in Tokyo*
38. Ibid.

CHAPTER 7 JIMMY RANEY'S ADVANCED ASYMMETRY & POLYMETRICS IN RECORDINGS

Fig. 7-8[39]

So far, we have shown how Jimmy creates polyrhythms by combining specific melodic structures; however, the guitar lesson example in Fig. 7-9 shows him doing this (after an initial 1 beat displacement) more by specific accents on a continuous line. Jimmy's rhythmic freedom comes from his comfort with accenting anywhere in the bar line (be sure to check out his exercises for this in the final chapter), and effectively weaving accents on and off the beat. Complex groupings such as 5's and 7's are ideal for achieving this and Jimmy seemed particularly fond of the latter grouping as several examples in the chapter and Fig. 7-9 over Rhythm changes would suggest.

Fig. 7-9

---

39. Raney, *Live in Tokyo*

THINGS TO THINK ABOUT

- Jimmy often used 6/4 and even 7/4 phrases, but did so in different ways:
  - Sequentially and rooted in blues or pentatonic scale material. (Fig. 7-3)
  - Sequentially but rooted in arpeggio material. (Fig. 7-8)
  - In minor scale sequences with an approach note that clearly defines the polyrhythmic grouping. (Fig. 7-2)
- Used mixed rhythmic groups with an eye towards creating sequences that resolved over larger bar range than typical 1 or 2 bar scope. (Figs. 7-5, 7-6)
- Accented in different asymmetric groupings spontaneously to create rhythmic tension and release. (Fig. 7-9)
- Left space, then came back in unexpected parts of the bar, creating anticipation and surprise; paired space with busier note passages to achieve contrast. (Fig. 7-7)

Section III

Primer and Practice on the Elements of Jimmy Raney's Language

INTRODUCTION TO SECTION III

Most established players (including Jimmy) recommend the tradition of learning to play solos of the masters. Transcribing Jimmy is not that difficult with the multitude of transcription aids available now. But many questions remain. What was his thinking process and methodology **behind** conceiving these ideas? And how can you use these transcribed ideas organically, globally, and creatively across different songs rather than simply playing them mechanically in their original contexts? To that end, this chapter will clearly identify the specific building blocks and phrasing patterns of Jimmy Raney's vocabulary and offer suggestions and exercises that will help students of Jimmy's art to build their own ideas, after gaining an understanding of these concepts.

I will be using samples across different Raney solos. Think of these sections as a snapshot of each piece of the puzzle that will eventually be built into the whole, which hopefully be clearer as you reach the end. It is important not to mistake this analytical process for the original ideas' conception, which is essentially "all-at once" (notes, phrasing, rhythm, and articulation). This is like any language learning. I'm just trying to run this at a slower speed for you.

CHAPTER 8: THE ESSENTIAL ELEMENTS OF JIMMY RANEY'S PHRASES

A: THE II-V LICKS

A typical "go-to" phrase that appears frequently in Jimmy's solos is the II minor scale fragment (1-2-3-4-5) or minor arpeggio (1-3-5-7) that connects to the 3rd of the V7 chord either directly via 5-7-3 enclosure or with an extra chromatic passing tone (7-5-#5-3). There are in essence the following:

Fig. 8-1 Minor scale to 3rd of V7

Fig. 8-2 Minor arpeggio to 3rd of V7 ("Round Midnite style" phrase)

Fig. 8-3 Minor scale plus chromatic enclosure

Fig. 8-4 Minor arpeggio plus chromatic enclosure

In Fig. 8-5 he plays the scalar start version on his solo intro to the ballad, "Body and Soul."

Fig. 8-5[40]

Fig. 8-5 is a double time lick in 16ths, but it would also work in eighths in a one chord per bar scenario.

---

40. Jimmy Raney, *Jimmy Raney Visits Paris, Vol. 1,* Vogue, 1954

CHAPTER 8 ESSENTIAL ELEMENTS: A. THE II-V LICKS

With the early targeting of the 3rd, it is sometimes necessary to extend the II-V and re-outline the progression. It was handled this way in Jimmy's solo to his tune, "Momentum" (aka "Motion") in Fig. 8-6.

(Note also how Jimmy uses a rest, eighth and 3 eighth note triplets on A-7 instead of 4 eighths for variety). Also note how the A-9 arpeggio (C∆7) goes to 3rd of D7 in the next bar.

Fig. 8-6[41]

Developing on the II again after the V7 is reached is a typical bebop technique for extending a chord progression, as well as building chords from the 3rd creating 9th chords. Fig. 8-7 shows a complete II-V-I with 9th chords built from a 3rd above the chord. Note how the chord symbols and arpeggios relate to each other and expand the linear vocabulary (D-9=Fmaj7, G9=B-7b5, Cmaj9=E-7).

Fig. 8-7 (II-V-I with 9th chords)

In Fig. 8-8, over his 2nd solo chorus to Cole Porter's "I Love You," bars 27-29, he plays a similar A-7 D7 phrase to Fig. 8-6 but starts it on beat 3 and pairs it with a slurred D9th phrase (similar to the V9 in Fig. 8-7, bar 2) and continues the 2-beat displacement thru the next bar:

Fig. 8-8[42]

In Fig. 8-9, in his solo to "What is This Thing Called Love" (bars 9-11), the II-V lick played combines both aspects of Fig. 8-7 and 8-8, in that it is harmonically and melodically similar to 8-7 (Minor scale and minor arpeggio reiteration) but it is rhythmically similar to 8-8 (2 beat rhythmic displacement).

---

41. Raney, *Momentum*
42. Raney, *The Influence*

Fig. 8-9[43]

The final II-V example in Fig. 8-10 on "How About You," bars 9-11, he uses the Fig. 8-2 II-V lick going directly from 7 to 3. This helps keep the strongly accented 3rd triplets going for this medium tempo swinger. The II-V is paired with one of Jimmy's favorite neighbor tone combinations (#9-b9-#7-1 on C7) — often started by an accented leap of a 7th against the grain as he's done here, creating surprise and excitement. We will get to that neighbor lick shortly.

Fig. 8-10[44]

B: INVERTED CHORD LINES

Bebop lines make ample use of inverted chordal phrases that originally came out of the Swing Era. One common phrase is the opening line of Fats Waller's "Honeysuckle Rose," which was a bebop vehicle for Charlie Parker in terms of the tune's chord structure.

Fig. 8-11 ("Honeysuckle Rose" by Fats Waller)

There are many jazz variations on this phrase but the heart of it is an inverted 7th arpeggio where the 2nd note goes down a 6th rather than up a 3rd:

Fig. 8-12 (Inverted 7th arpeggio procedure)

As we have discussed, chords a 3rd apart are related, so the inverted line can be used for a major chord or the minor chord a m3 below (Bb and G-7 respectively in Fig. 8-12). Also, an inverted line can be used on a different chord quality as in 8-13:

---

43. Raney, *Raney '81*
44. Raney, *Live in Tokyo*

CHAPTER 8 ESSENTIAL ELEMENTS: B. INVERTED CHORD LINES

Fig. 8-13 (Dominant 7th)

Figs. 8-14 ("I Could Write a Book," 2nd chorus, bars 14-15) and 8-15 ("Double Image," bars 23-24) show how Jimmy uses the inverted dominant 7 in context (see circled). The inverted arpeggio paired with ii-V enclosures in sequence is a frequent formula in Jimmy's long harmonic lines, targeting 3rds in a kind of up-down weaving fashion:

Fig. 8-14[45]

Fig. 8-15[46]

Of course, you can do more than invert one note downward as in II-V "Honeysuckle" style lines. Note order can be changed as well. In Fig. 8-16, the 2nd and 3rd notes (see connecting lines) are reversed in order in addition to being inverted as in previous examples:

Fig. 8-16 (Inverted and order change)

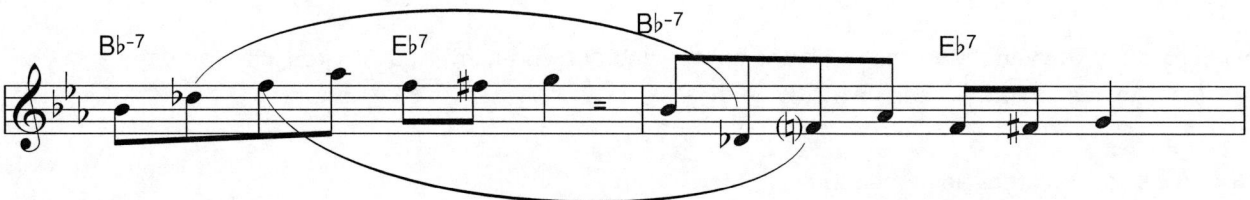

Fig. 8-17 shows a common Charlie Parker style diminished lick that could also be looked at as a note order change (starting with B in the downward G7 arpeggio instead of "D") or perhaps its more common classification: a broken chord.

---

45. Raney, *Wistaria*
46. Jimmy Raney, *Jimmy Raney Quartet 1954,* New Jazz, 1954

Fig. 8-17

The chord inversion procedure can also be reversed. A downward note can invert upward as shown in Fig. 8-18:

Fig. 8-18 (Downward interval reversed upward)

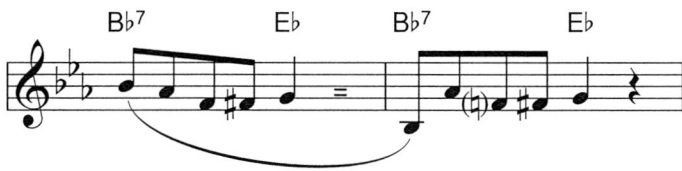

C: AUXILIARY TONES AND MELODIC INTERVALS

Passing (PT), neighbor tones (NT) and turns - also known as *auxiliary* tones — are like the glue that holds together typical bebop phrases. There are hundreds possible in combination, but certain ones are favored, and Jimmy has particular ones that he used frequently, often in conjunction with the scalar and chordal lines we have discussed thus far. You have already seen how Jimmy uses upward chromatic passing tones to connect to the 3rd of the V7. Generally, the II-V enclosure process is a combined neighbor tone and a passing tones sequence, where the target tone is approached from above, below, and then the target tone is arrived at by chromatic passing tones (see Fig. 8-18).

The target can be approached from below with neighbors but generally the passing tone still approaches chromatically upward as in Jimmy's solo to "Have You Met Miss Jones" in Fig. 8-19 (measure 21).

Passing Tones (PT)

Fig. 8-19[47]

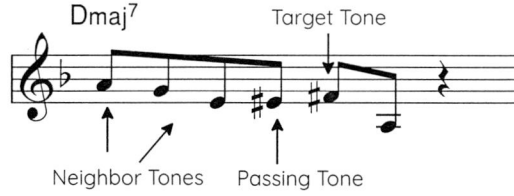

---

47. Raney, *Visits Paris, Vol. 2*

Fig. 8-20 (Jimmy's 2nd solo chorus on "I Love You," bars 27-28)[48]

Jimmy also likes to use quick passing or neighbor tones between the 5th and the root or to embellish a harmonic interval (a note that implies a harmony but is only 2 notes). In Fig. 8-21 Jimmy does this in sequence over his "The Flag is Up" (bars 1-3) where the passing tone is repeated but the upper tone moves up and down with the harmony.

Fig. 8-21[49]

Another use of the PT is for Jimmy's typical strong tonic statements often to end or begin a section as in Fig. 8-22 over "Nowhere," bars 16-17 (see circled notes). The upward passing tone provides the extra connecting note from 3rd to 5th or 5th to tonic usually.

Fig. 8-22[50]

A PT combination from m3 to 5 is also a typical phrase he uses on a blues solo in below Fig. 8-23 and rhythm changes (see Fig. 7-7) or standards.

Fig. 8-23 ("Blue Duke" solo, bars 3-4)[51]

---

48. Raney, *The Influence*
49. Jimmy Raney, *Jimmy Raney featuring Bob Brookmeyer*, ABC Paramount, 1956
50. Raney, *Play Along*, Vol. 20
51. Kenny Burrell/*Jimmy Raney, Two Guitars*, Prestige, 1957

Neighbor Tones (NT)

Jimmy frequently uses neighbor tones on #4-6-5 or Δ7 9 1. On later records, Jimmy often abandoned the long eighth note solo breaks he had used earlier in favor of simpler developing motives that use dotted quarters and/or neighbor tone sequences. Both 8-24 ("What is Thing Called Love," bars 1-6) and 8-25 ("My Shining Hour," bars 1-6) use this technique and are from the same record. 8-24 uses Δ7 9 1 and a phrase development technique called *diminution* that will be discussed later — where notes move closer together and quicken in value. 8-25 starts with #4 6 1 and continues in a C triad neighbor tone sequence in dotted quarters (the changes are mostly irrelevant here and are not indicated).

Fig. 8-24[52]

Fig. 8-25[53]

Turns

Fig. 8-26 shows a turn sequence on the 5th, root and 3rd popularized by Charlie Parker (the note "turned" on is the middle note. In this case B, E and G#) solo over "The Song is You" (2nd chorus, bars 1-2).

Fig. 8-26[54]

In addition to familiar turn sequences are the use of "Chopin-esque" chromatic lower turns (usually pivoting at the chord's 5th below the interval). This particular phrase was really one that everybody played in the swing era, through the bebop era (in particular Sonny Stitt) and beyond. See Jimmy's solos:

---

52. Raney, *Raney '81*
53. Ibid.
54. Raney, *The Master*

CHAPTER 8 ESSENTIAL ELEMENTS: C. AUXILIARY TONES AND MELODIC INTERVALS

Fig. 8-27 ("My Shining Hour," bars 13-14)[55]

Fig. 8-28 ("Nobody Else but Me," bars 22-24)[56]

Fig. 8-29 ("Pennies from Heaven," solo 4th chorus bars 1-2)[57]

Multiple NT & PT licks

Jimmy's passing tones could be combined, almost bordering on chromatic. Fig. 8-30 shows a frequent phrase of Jimmy's, where there is a chromatic tone on every step (except C♯ in this example). But again, this technique was not new, but rather something picked up from Bud Powell. Jimmy has always displayed the proper balance between his more unique phrases and those borrowed from his influences.

---

55. Raney, *Raney '81*
56. Raney, *Brookmeyer*
57. Raney, *Visits Paris, Vol. 1*

Fig. 8-30 ("The Flag Is Up," 2nd solo chorus, bars 1-2)[58]

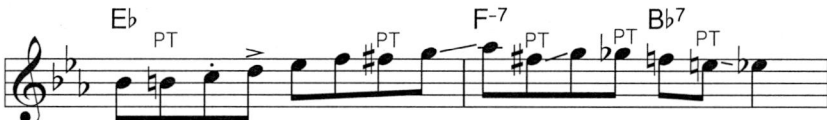

Jimmy's passing tones could be surprising in terms of the chord played against. A frequent trick of his was to play on the major 3rd of minor chord first before arriving to the minor 3rd via chromatic passing tone and neighbor tone enclosure as in Fig. 8-31:

Fig. 8-31 ("Invention" solo, bars 14-15)[59]

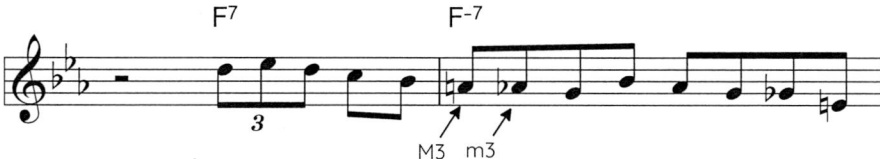

Sometimes "avoid notes" reflected his across the bar line concept where he was not quite done with the previous chord until later in the next bar. This occurs two times within the first 12 measures of his solo to "Stella by Starlight." In Fig. 8-32 he still is playing on A7 alt on the first beat of the C-7 bar. In Fig. 8-33 he plays the same thing but also adds unusual neighbor tones to get to the 5th of D-7 chord:

Fig. 8-32 ("Stella by Starlight" solo, bars 2-3)[60]

Fig. 8-33 (same solo, bars 10-11)

The "Stella by Starlight" examples show Jimmy Raney's most frequent phrase connectors: **multiple neighbor tone** combinations (also known as "enclosures") starting on the #9. The combination most frequently used is #9-♭9-6-Δ7-9-1 (the Δ7-9-1 could also be considered #4-6-1 of target chord). They are similar in shape to the inverted chord lines discussed earlier.

---

58. Raney, *Brookmeyer*
59. Raney, *Play Along, Vol. 29*
60. Jimmy Raney, *Jimmy Raney Ensemble featuring Phil Woods,* New Jazz, 1954

There is some variability in the 2nd interval although the more frequent seems to be a major 3rd. For example, the 2 NT phrases in 8-32 and 8-33 begin similarly but the target notes end up being different (B♭ and A respectively). The neighbor tone combination, in addition to creating melodic elaboration and dissonance, also creates a cross cutting rhythm, often in 5/8.

Fig. 8-34 is a similar note combination performed a half step higher. Note how the dominant 7th "avoid" note on the major 7th is of little consequence. But also note that it has the same B♭ target as Fig. 8-32 despite it starting a half-step higher. This shows that the procedure is not completely fixed.

Fig. 8-34 ("Double Image," 2 bar break)[61]

The note combination is also present in 8-35 and 8-36:

Fig. 8-35 ("Have You Met Miss Jones" solo, bars 27-28)[62]

Fig. 8-36 ("Momentum" solo, 6th chorus, bars 15-16)[63]

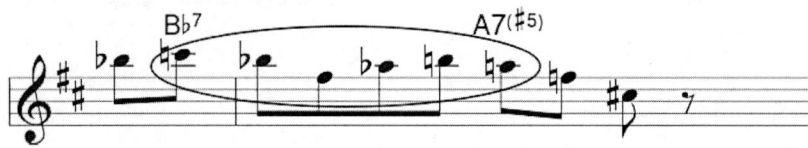

The multiple neighbor pattern is played twice in II-V sequence on Fig. 8-37 and its cross-cutting rhythmic aspect is clearly understood as it creates a 5/4 phrase by delaying the 2nd II-V by a beat. In fact, there are really four implied 5/8 phrases when you identify each minor 7th arpeggio and neighbor tone combination (see slurs):

---

61. Raney, *Quartet '54*
62. Raney, *Visits Paris, Vol. 2*
63. Raney, *Momentum*

Fig. 8-37 ("Invention" solo, 4th chorus, bars 30-32)[64]

This great line features several multiple neighbor tone combinations over a tricky turnaround. Notice how the B7 harmony begins a little early in bar 13. So modern for its time!

Fig. 8-38 ("Everything I've Got Belongs to You" solo, bars 13-16)[65]

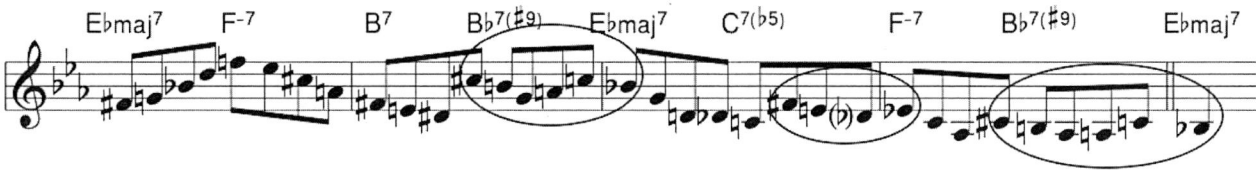

As Jimmy's career progressed, he used passing and neighbor tone combinations more and more by ear leading to frequent "apparent" contradictions to existing chords. It wasn't for lack of attention; it was simply that the line itself and the target tone (however he got there) was paramount, and that's how he heard it.

---

64. Raney, *Play Along, Vol. 29*
65. Red Norvo, *Red Norvo Trio*, Prestige, 1954

CHAPTER 8A-C EXERCISES: II-V'S, INVERTED CHORDS, AUXILIARY TONES

Now that we have covered a substantial amount of Raney type phrasing material, let's try to create some of our own solo phrases based on some of these models. I will start you off with the first one to the familiar standard "How High the Moon" in Ex. 8-1. Continue with the example in the same style and try to put in a chapter concept I did not include. Remember that you can use you own phrases as long as you give a nod in the direction of the material being covered. This is the point — don't obliterate your own vocabulary, but rather augment it with the new material and try to fit into your overall style as seamlessly as you can. This may require writing out the notes and editing. Have fun with it!

Exercise 8-1   (Solo over "How High the Moon," first 12 bars)

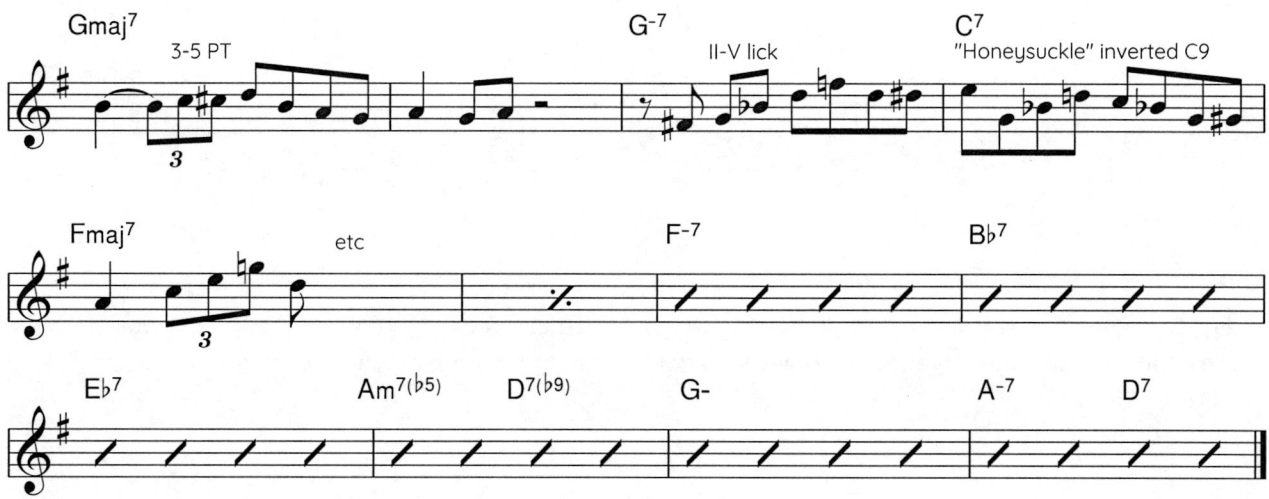

Exercise 8-2   (Raney neighbor tone exercise from Fig. 8-37)

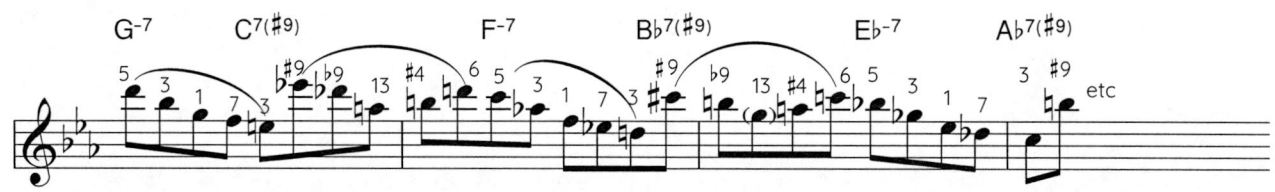

In exercise 8-2, continue the II-V melodic pattern played by Jimmy in whole steps (from Fig. 8-37) until you reach the chord at the top of the progression. When mastered, take the progression up a half step to A♭-7 and repeat the same process to get to all the possible II-V chords. This progression is in 5/4 so the reader is encouraged to play with a metronome that keeps track of 1.

In this whole step progression, the II-V returns to beat 1 on the B-7 chord of the sequence. There is one note change in the original line on the 2nd V7♯9 to make it consistent (see note "G" in parenthesis).

D: MAJOR CHORD CONCEPTS

This section ties up some of the material from the previous II-V-I section as it relates to the I chord, where examples were given, but not gone in-depth. It also pertains to major chord material that is apart from the II-V-I progression. Jimmy's particular penchant on major is the #11 (see Fig. 8-39):

Fig. 8-39 ("Out of Nowhere" solo, bar 17)[66]

During the period from '52-54, Jimmy's compositions (e.g., Signal, Motion, and Lee) and improvisations had some of the outward harmonic characteristics and feeling of the "Cool" and "Tristano" schools, sometimes using broad weaving upper structures and complex arpeggio sequences over major chords with regularity. This characteristic lessened to a degree later where his programmed licks gave way to more following his ear. But he did have complex signature phrases that you can clearly hear throughout his recorded career.

Fig. 8-40 is a typical weaving arpeggio phrase he used on "Pennies from Heaven" on his solo break to move between the I and II major chords (D and E) to achieve the #11 sound. Fig. 8-41 uses a similar procedure to begin the 2nd chorus but returns to a regular D major triad.

Fig. 8-40[67]

Fig. 8-41[68]

A I-II triad sequence is used in Fig. 8-42 to begin Jimmy's 2nd chorus solo to his tune, "Double Image" also from 1954. In this one he weaves between Eb6 (I) F(II) and Bb6(V) arpeggios:

---

66. Red Norvo, *Red Norvo Trio*, Prestige, 1954
67. Raney, *Visits Paris Vol. 1*
68. Ibid.

CHAPTER 8 ESSENTIAL ELEMENTS: **D.** MAJOR CHORD CONCEPTS

Fig. 8-42[69]

He starts out playing a nearly identical phrase on "Everything I've Got Belongs to You" in Fig. 8-43 (bars 17-19), but then on the 9th note it changes and outlines VII and III arpeggios, adding more harmonic complexity:

Fig. 8-43[70]

He plays a similar complex arpeggio sequence (I, II, III) over his famous tune, "Motion," but uses a Vmaj7 arpeggio (Amaj7) instead of VII (D) as in Fig. 8-43. Again, he plays in an up-down weaving arpeggio style at the end of the first chorus:

Fig. 8-44[71]

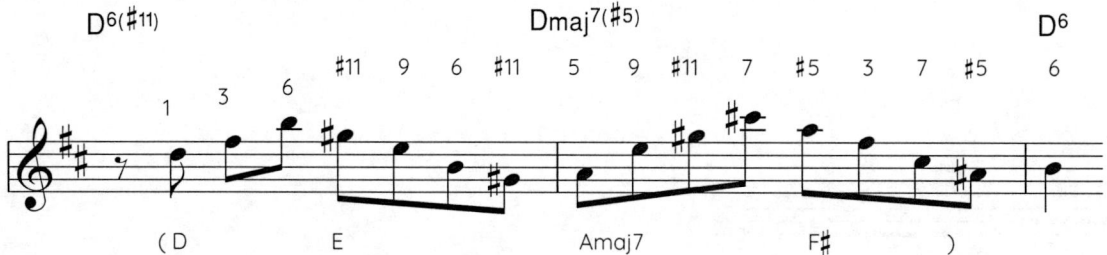

Jimmy has numerous examples of the modern approach to the major chord in his playing with Red Norvo. Given the contrast with the more swing oriented style of Norvo and material (e.g. "Crazy Rhythm," "Everything I've Got," and "Out of Nowhere"), Jimmy's contemporary approach and feel was accentuated even more so. The length of the repeated arpeggio on G triad over F major makes you wonder if Jimmy was making a practical joke on the morning bugle song, "Reveille." Especially when he quotes the American Folk song "Dixie" right after it (see Figs. 8-45-46).

---

69. Raney, *Quartet '54*
70. Ibid.
71. Jimmy Raney, *Jimmy Raney Plays*, Prestige, 1953

Fig. 8-45 ("Crazy Rhythm," solo break)[72]

Fig. 8-46[73]

Jimmy's #11 "persistence" is also in evidence on this cut from the same Norvo sessions:

Fig. 8-47 ("Everything I've Got Belongs to You" solo, bars 41-44)[74]

Still, Jimmy just as often followed Charlie Parker's model when it came to traversing major chords. Shortly after the "bugle call" figure from Fig. 8-46, Jimmy played a turn popularized by Charlie Parker (quoted earlier in Fig. 8-26 over "The Song Is You" in the section on "turns").

Fig. 8-48 ("Crazy Rhythm" solo, bars 6-7)[75]

He played the same turn in F in Fig. 8-49 but began it a beat later:

---

72. Norvo Trio, '54
73. Ibid.
74. Ibid.
75. Ibid.

Fig. 8-49 ("Have You Met Miss Jones" solo, 2nd chorus, bars 8-9)[76]

Turns in combination with scalar and arpeggio material were a common device Jimmy used. Again, this was built on Charlie Parker's model. In Fig. 8-50 over "Motion" beginning his 2nd chorus, he uses a scalar walk-up, turn and major triad.

Fig. 8-50[77]

In Fig. 8-51, in the 2nd chorus of the same solo (bars 7-8), Jimmy again uses the turn with triad arpeggio. But he also uses neighboring material from the V7 chord prior to set it up.

Fig. 8-51[78]

Certain material that Jimmy used over major chord was "in the air" and very related to popular song. A frequent phrase he uses is related to both "Zing Goes the Strings of My Heart" and/or "Them There Eyes." Basically, it is a major scale fragment 1235 and embellishes on the 6 as well. They are demonstrated on Figs. 52-53. This usually serves as set-up material for more complex passages.

---

76. Raney, *Visits Paris, Vol. 2*
77. Raney, *Jimmy Raney Plays*
78. Ibid.

Fig. 8-52 ("Momentum" solo, 3rd chorus, bars 19-20)[79]

Fig. 8-53 ("Alone Together" solo, bars 27-28)[80]

Although not exactly the same (the G and B♭ are reversed, #5 is added as well as neighbor tone, D), it's obvious that Fig. 8-54 is a phrase very much along the same lines.

Fig. 8-54 ("Bout You & Me," bars 25-26)[81]

A common jazz phrase is what I call the "Misty" variant which plays off the opening melody of the song on 5-3-7-5-6. It has become an extremely common jazz cliché, has a certain definitiveness about it and Jimmy likes to use it as well (see Fig. 8-55):

Fig. 8-55 ("The Best Thing for You," bars 16-17)[82]

---

79. Raney, *Momentum*
80. Jimmy Raney, *Stolen Moments,* Steeplechase, 1979
81. Raney, *Play Along, Vol. 20*
82. Red Norvo, *Red Norvo Trio,* Brunswick, 1953

CHAPTER 8 ESSENTIAL ELEMENTS:

E: MINOR CHORD CONCEPTS

Much of the minor chord- scale content is contained within II-V-I studies. Although there might be overlap, this material has more to do with extended minor II changes or tonic minor passages.

Minor moving 7th

The moving 7th is again adopted from the Parker model. It deals with outlining the extended minor II chord with a guide tone moving from the root to the 6th, which becomes the 3rd of the connecting V7.

Fig. 8-56 ("Motion" solo, 2nd chorus, bars 9-10)[83]

This is a more extended moving 7th example of Jimmy's over a 4 bar G-7 C7 change:

Fig. 8-57 ("Scrapple from the Apple" solo, bars 1-4)[84]

This is an example where the motion is in the outer voice and deftly integrated within the overall line:

Fig. 8-58 ("How About You," 2nd solo chorus, bars 18-19)[85]

Here's an example that reverses the direction of the 7th:

Fig. 8-59 ("Too Marvelous for Words" solo, bars 9-11)[86]

---

83. Raney, *Jimmy Raney Plays*
84. Jimmy Raney, *Here's that Rainy Day*, Ahead, 1980
85. Raney, *Live in Tokyo*
86. Raney, *Visits Paris, Vol. 2*

5-123 scalar phrase

Jimmy frequently plays this common "up-to-tonic" approach minor scale jazz phrase shown in Fig. 8-60 and 8-61 (though often in major too). It probably has its roots in J.S. Bach melodies. As you can see, he typically applies this phrase on different beats and speeds for variety.

Fig. 8-60 ("Just Friends" solo, 2nd chorus, bars 25-26)[87]

Fig. 8-61 ("Morning of the Carnival" solo, bars 24-25)[88]

In this example, the 5-123 scale pattern is used in sequence and the tune itself is transposed to the challenging key of A♭ minor:

Fig. 8-62 ("Yesterdays" solo intro)[89]

Another frequent phrase pattern is where the lower 5th moves upward to the 6th. It's a very well-known jazz cliché used in a variety of contexts and tunes. In Fig. 8-63 Jimmy uses the phrase over C- from G to A:

Fig. 8-63 ("Get Out of Town" solo, 3rd chorus, bar 6)[90]

---

87. Raney, *Momentum*
88. Jimmy Raney, *Two Jims and Zoot,* Mainstream, 1964
89. Raney, *Visits Paris Vol. 1*
90. Raney, *The Influence*

CHAPTER 8 ESSENTIAL ELEMENTS: E. MINOR CHORD CONCEPTS

The previous pattern is reversed with a downward moving 5th on Jimmy's tune, the 2-guitar counterpoint, "Minor" (based on changes to "Bernie's Tune") although the 5th is really moving to the dominant 7th of B♭7 (see Fig. 8-64)

Fig. 8-64[91]

5-6-7-1

Jimmy also uses a strong scalar ascension to the root in his minor chord patterns. The pattern could be deemed the upper portion of the melodic minor scale but in most cases, Jimmy also includes non-scale tones. Fig. 8-65 below his solo over "Just One of those Things" (bars 48-51) reflects his Bud Powell influence.

Fig. 8-65[92]

Fig. 8-66 ("Darn that Dream" solo, bar 3)[93]

Polyrhythmic minor scales

Jimmy frequently uses minor scales sequentially and polyrhythmically thru changes. This was an example used earlier with minor scale fragments:

(Fig. 5-7, from Chapter 5)

---

91. Raney, *Quartet '54*
92. Norvo, *Trio '54*
93. Jimmy Raney, *Strings and Swings*, Muse, 1969

Common jazz practice typically applies melodic minor scales modally, but Jimmy often uses Dorian in these situations (sometimes starting with lower N.T.), characteristically leaning into the 6-7 of the Dorian scale with an accented slur. When he uses melodic minor, it tends to be when the minor moves to Lydian chord. You can see this approach in Fig. 8-67:

Fig. 8-67 ("Just Friends" solo 2nd chorus, bars 25-30)[94]

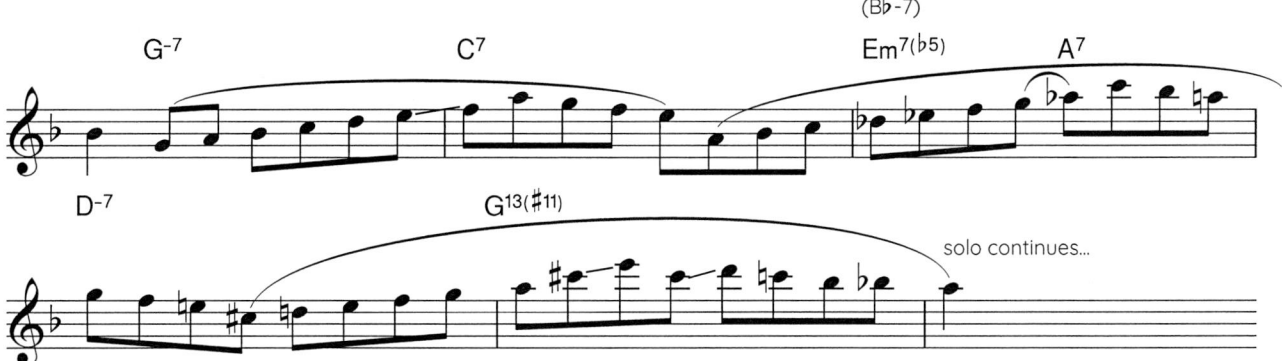

F: DOMINANT CHORD CONCEPTS

As a prologue to the study of dominant chord related scales, I don't think that Jimmy thought very much about them in terms of solo conception – at least consciously. This is quoted from Jimmy in a well-known lecture from 1993 on this topic:

"We didn't have it worked out like Jamey (Aebersold) and those guys...I learned scales because the classical teachers assume you are going to play classical music and ... scales are very helpful. I think I just did it on my own . . . To be very honest with you, playing scales and modes or 7th scales... in the last analysis is here (points to his ear). Your ear guides you or fails to guide you as E.B. White says about prose and all the rules of grammar and syntax ain't gonna help if you don't hear it . . . It's good to know all that stuff but don't think it will make you play."

But there does seem to be evidence in the next examples that he knew scales a little better than he let on. And to look at when he *did* use scales provides an interesting foil against when he avoided them in favor of melodic considerations or superimposed harmony. Regardless of whether Jimmy's conception had anything to do with scales or if the commonality with scales is coincidental, the student ultimately can incorporate the ideas in whichever system best suits his or her learning style, or no system at all. In a word, It's all good.

½ W Diminished

a. ♭9♯9 combo

This combination was mentioned in the very first chapter on improving line. Jimmy refers to this combination as a *suspension* because of the inevitable resolution to a ½ step below the ♭9. He uses it with such frequency that it should be considered fundamental to his linear architecture. The scale basis of the combo is most likely based in ½ W diminished because of his consistent use of natural fifth prior (as opposed ♯5 in altered dominant) In any case, in Fig. 8-68 it occurs twice within the same phrase:

---

94. Raney, *Momentum*

Fig. 8-68 ("Momentum" solo, bars 24-27)[95]

In the 2nd chorus of "Momentum" solo (bars 5-6), he uses this combination several times over the same changes and one other time over the modulation to B♭ but it is slightly displaced rhythmically from the previous example:

Fig. 8-69[96]

In Fig. 8-70 the combo figure occurs on beat 3 to 4 and resolves to the 3rd of A♭maj7:

Fig. 8-70 ("There Will Never Be Another You" solo, bars 24-25)[97]

Figs. 8-71 and 8-72 show how Jimmy likes to string together the V7♭9#9 combination with the I major #4-6-5 neighbor tone pattern:

Fig. 8-71 ("The Song is You" solo, bars 4-5)[98]

Fig. 8-72 (Same solo, bars 32-33)[99]

---

95. Raney, *Momentum*
96. Ibid.
97. Raney, *The Influence*
98. Stan Getz, *Stan Getz Quintet,* Birdland Sessions, Fresh Sounds, 1952
99. Ibid.

There are numerous other examples of the ♭9♯9 combination in Jimmy's solos and it is really not necessary to point out every one of them, as I'm sure the principle of its use in dominant suspension and resolution is clear from the prior examples in this book.

b. Upper Structure VI triad (V13♭9)

The V7 13♭9 chord can be considered as derived from the ½ W diminished scale because of the unique occurrence of that combination of those extended tones within the scale. In Fig. 8-73 on his solo to "The Song is You" (bar 8), he uses an E triad over a G7 chord:

Fig. 8-73[100]

This VI triad concept was developed early as these '53-'54 solos show:

Fig. 8-74 ("Signal" solo, 2nd chorus, bar 10)[101]

Fig. 8-75 ("Too Marvelous for Words" solo, 2nd chorus, bar 4)[102]

And even earlier in this bridge section of the '52 version of "The Song is You," Jimmy utilizes the upper structure VI triad in sequence:

---

100. Raney, *The Master*
101. Raney, *Jimmy Raney Plays*
102. Raney, *Visits Paris, Vol. 2*

CHAPTER 8 ESSENTIAL ELEMENTS: F. DOMINANT CHORD CONCEPTS

Fig. 8-76[103]

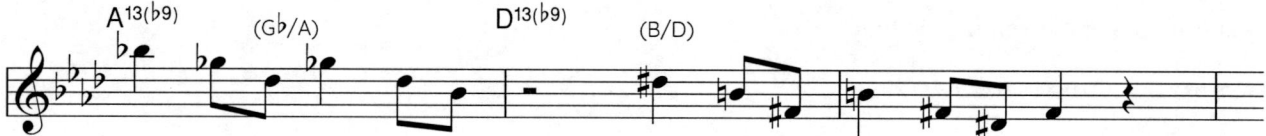

Here is an example over his solo to "Everything I've Got Belongs to You" (bars 9-10), where he combines the ♭9#9 scalar aspect with the VI triad concept, reinforcing the sound of diminished:

Fig. 8-77[104]

c. Upper Structure ♭V triad (V7♭9♭5)

The ♭V U.S. triad is shared by the ½ W diminished and altered dominant scales, however in Fig. 8-78, the A♭ triad along with the use of A natural clearly implies diminished. Actually, the functional designation in relation to the tonic is ♭II (e.g., A♭ is ♭V in relation to D7 but is ♭II in relation to tonic G major). He uses that in Fig. 8-78 in his solo to "It Could Happen to You" in bar 16:

Fig. 8-78[105]

Here the ♭V arpeggio is used over F7 on his solo to "Cherokee" (bars 30-31). This example is also quoted in Fig. 8-100 in the ♭VI-7 ♭II7 section as well because the clear application of that substitution in the passage.

Fig. 8-79[106]

d. Upper structure #IIm7 (♭IIIm7)

This C-7 F7 progression over his solo to "Just Friends" (bars 31-32) implies a G-7 to G#-7 upper structure motion:

---

103. Getz, *Birdland '52*
104. Norvo, *Trio '54*
105. Raney, *The Influence*
106. Raney, *Visits Paris, Vol. 2*

Fig. 8-80[107]

This phrase combines the #IIm7 and the VI polychords:

Fig. 8-81 ("Signal "solo, bars 8-9)[108]

e. Sequence and scale patterns

Figs. 8-82 and 8-83 are typical diminished pattern sequences, which as a general rule, Jimmy seemed to avoid. Note also that below example is an early one from 1954.

Fig. 8-82 ("The Best Thing for You," bars 25-28)[109]

Fig. 8-83 ("Too Marvelous for Words "solo, bar 28)[110]

Figs. 8-84 shows a clear E ½ W diminished scale over the VI7 chord, which is unusual for Jimmy because he is generally more inclined to presage the tones of target minor.

---

107. Raney, *Momentum*
108. Raney, *Jimmy Raney Plays*
109. Norvo, *Trio '54*
110. Raney, *Visits Paris, Vol. 2*

Fig. 8-84 ("It Could Happen to You" solo, bars 28-29)[111]

Altered Dominant

a. The "descending altered lick"

Jimmy used altered harmony on his dominant chords quite often. Figs. 8-85 and 8-86 shows a typical descending altered dominant lick that in some circles is referred to as "the lick" because of its pervasive use as a jazz cliché.

Fig. 8-85 ("Just Friends" solo, 2nd chorus, bar 4)[112]

Fig. 8-86 ("Stella by Starlight" solo, 3rd chorus, bar 1)[113]

Fig. 8-87 ("Everything I've Got Belongs to You" solo, bars 24-25)[114]

Fig. 8-88 uses the altered dominant lick in sequence. Note also the altered - Lydian dominant inverse relationship on the tritone relative chord.

---

111. Raney, *The Influence*
112. Raney, *Momentum*
113. Raney, *Strings & Swings*
114. Norvo, *Trio '54*

Fig. 8-88 ("Signal" solo, 4th chorus, bars 2-5)[115]

b. The "Barney Kessel lick"

In the quoted lecture Jimmy also mentions his admiration for Barney Kessel, given his slightly elder status and established presence on the jazz scene when Jimmy was just a teenager. Says Jimmy:

He played a beautiful solo on "Grabtown Grapple." He played one lick I played all my life (plays lick). I stole that from him (laughs)."

This was the original solo lick Barney played on the 1945 recording with Artie Shaw's Gramercy Five. It's a very wide sweeping inventive lick using a ♯5 and ♭9.

Fig. 8-89[116]

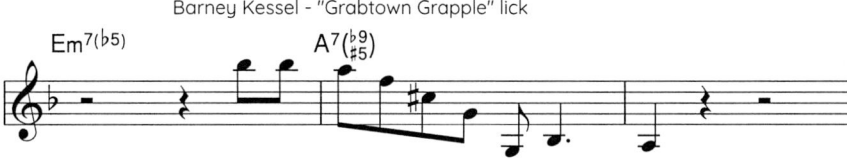

The sweeping altered lick that Jimmy refers to in his playing, though similar, is a little different from Kessel's original. It doesn't use the 7th or the ♭9 and it also introduces a ♭5 in addition to the augmented fifth, which points to altered dominant as the source.

Fig. 8-90 ("Just Friends" solo, bar 27)[117]

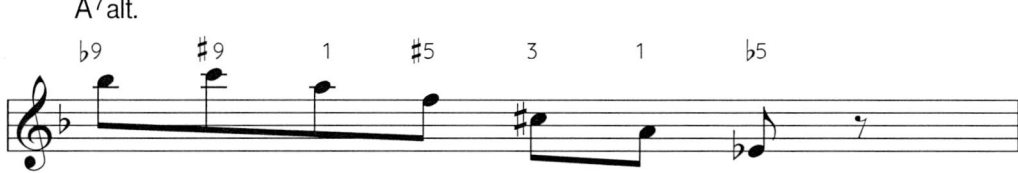

Jimmy played a similar lick in Fig. 8-91 (next page).

---

115. Raney, *Jimmy Raney Plays*
116. Artie Shaw, *Artie Shaw and His Gramercy Five*, RCA Victor, 1945
117. Raney, *Momentum*

CHAPTER 8 ESSENTIAL ELEMENTS: F. DOMINANT CHORD CONCEPTS

Fig. 8-91 ("Anthropology" solo, 3rd chorus, bars 30-31)[118]

As well as here:

Fig. 8-92 ("Strike Up the Band" solo, bar 27)[119]

♭vi-♭II7 Substitution

From the early days of his career, Jimmy has used the II-V7 tritone substitute, ♭VI-♭II7, and he was among the earliest jazz artists to do so and with such frequency. Because of the ♭VI minor scale conception, it is related to the altered dominant scale, but technically this is simply Dorian on ♭VI. You find this tritone substitution frequently in the Red Norvo trio recordings from 1954. I think this advanced chord substitution (in addition to all his other polychordal approaches) drove both jazz fans and contemporaries to his playing at that time.

Fig. 8-93 ("Out of Nowhere," solo break)[120]

Fig. 8-94 ("Just One of Those Things" solo, bars 5-7)[121]

As evidenced in "Out of Nowhere" example he liked to set up this tritone II-V tonality in the opening break. He does it here again on his 1956 recording of "Strike Up the Band."

---

118. Raney, *Live in Tokyo*
119. Raney, *Three Attitudes*
120. Norvo, *Trio '54*
121. Ibid.

Fig. 8-95 ("Strike Up the Band," solo break)[122]

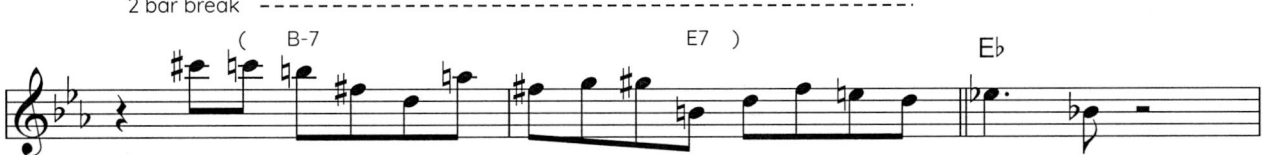

Later on in the solo he uses the tritone II-V technique again over F-7 B♭7. Notice how it smoothly sets up the ½ step II-V pattern to A♭.

Fig. 8-96 (same solo, 3rd chorus, bars 5-8)[123]

In these measures of the same solo, he uses the ♭VI-♭II7 to get to the A♭ chord:

Fig. 8-97 (same solo, 2nd chorus, bars 7-9)[124]

A similar approach is used here over the same change on a record from the same year:

Fig. 8-98 ("Nobody Else but Me" solo, bars 22-24)[125]

---

122. Raney, *Three Attitudes*
123. Ibid.
124. Ibid.
125. Raney, *Brookmeyer*

This ♭VI-II7 line builds at the tail end of G7 which begins with the ♭9#9 combo:

Fig. 8-99 ("Just Friends" solo, bars 13-14)[126]

Fig. 8-100 is a related example, where ♭VI-♭II7 progression is used on the II7 and then continues to ♭II of the key. In strict functional analysis this passage is II-V of ♭II before arriving on I.

Fig. 8-100 ("Cherokee" solo, bars 25-31)[127]

This final ♭VI-♭II7 Raney lick is a classic:

Fig. 8-101 ("Anthropology," guitar-drum trades)[128]

The lick in Fig. 8-101 is most likely Jimmy's invention. He played it as early as 1957 on "Suite for Guitar Quintet" on the cut "Miracle on Main Street" in the guitar solo section (see Fig. 8-102).

Fig. 8-102[129]

---

126. Raney, *Momentum*
127. Raney, *Visits Paris, Vol. 2*
128. Raney, *Live in Tokyo*
129. Raney, *Strings & Swings*

V7 substitutes: diminished and non-V7 polychords

Aside from V7♭9 substitutes, there are other diminished progressions in jazz (e.g., I°- I, ♭III°- II, #IV°- I) probably originating from the sounds of classical pedal point. Jimmy's lines outlining the progressions C-7-A/C# -D-7, C-7-Fmaj#5-B♭ and B♭° - B♭ major are all related to this alternate diminished motion.

In chapter 2, on the subject of harmonic dislocation, Jimmy introduced a standard bebop lick that utilizes the A triad (circled) pass-through chord in the opening of "rhythm changes":

Fig. 2-9

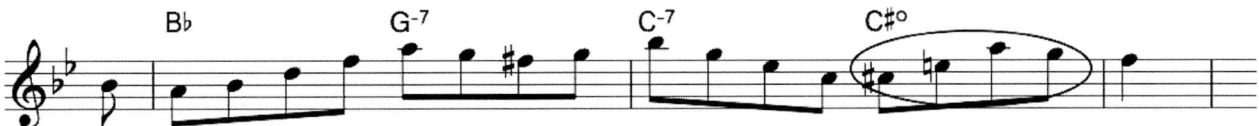

In of itself, this is nothing major, C#°- Dmin (B♭/D) is simply a variation of A7- Dmin. However, because of the interchangeability between I (B♭) and III (D-7), it does create interesting possibilities with chords from technically different dominant/diminished families (i.e., F7♭9 and A7♭9) being shared and consequently non-traditional chords being used over a II-V-I (for example Fmaj7#5 instead of F7). The implied A-B♭ upward triad motion of Fig. 2-8 is now in the chord progression mix and serves to ground conceptually some of Jimmy's ascending major chord explorations at the beginning of this section.

In these four examples, Jimmy applied the ascending diminished maj7 triad concept (more or less) conventionally, and the harmonic interpretation - whether VII triad occurs over dominant or root — just depends on where you draw the bar line.

Fig. 8-103 ("Momentum" solo, bars 38-40) [130]

Fig. 8-104 ("Momentum" solo, 3rd chorus, bars 5-7)[131]

---

130. Raney, *Momentum*
131. Ibid.

Fig. 8-105 ("Momentum" solo, bars 10-12)[132]

Fig. 8-106 ("Cross Your Heart" solo, bars 14-15)[133]

The implied triad motion (A♭-A-B♭) in Fig. 8-107 doesn't quite jive with a typical II-V-I progression or diminished substitute because the diminished maj7 is occurring on V7 (A/B♭). Nevertheless, it sounds conventional because it is built with similar upward triad motion as the previous examples but applied in a polychordal manner. It could also relate to the diminished I triad family possibly (E♭ G♭ A D).

Fig. 8-107 ("Double Image" solo, bars 15-16)[134]

It should be noted that the "weaving polychord technique" and the diminished substitute triad mentioned thus far could easily be interpretated as **an implied pedal point.** In fact, imagining a pedal tonic or dominant pedal under the lines discussed earlier in Figs. 8-43-44 helps make the line approach clearer. It's application near the end of the form on the "Motion" solo further reinforces its interpretation as pedal point, given this is where pedal point most frequently occurs.

---

132. Raney, *Momentum*
133. Jimmy Raney, *Jimmy Raney 1955,* Prestige, 1955
134. Raney, *Quartet '54*

CHAPTER 8D-F EXERCISES: MAJOR, MINOR AND DOMINANT CHORDS

Let's look at some the materials covered on Jimmy Raney's approaches to *major, minor,* and *dominant* chords.

In **major** chords, Jimmy often used sophisticated chord color like the ♯11 and the ♯5. One of his techniques discussed was weaving upper structure triads in sequence especially in tonic or dominant pedal point sections. This is an example given earlier on "Motion," Fig. 8-44:

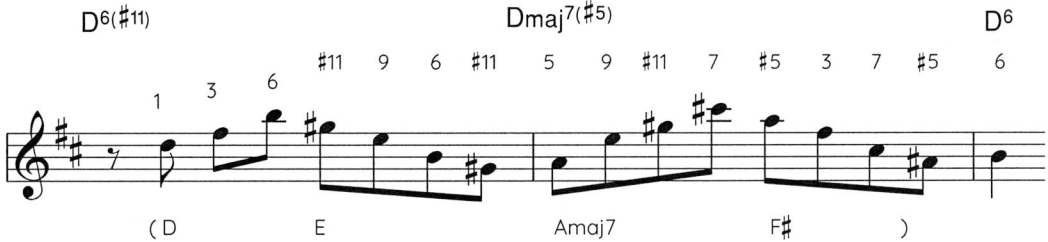

The original tune this is based Is "You Stepped Out of a Dream" in C major.

Play this lick in the turnaround 4 bars before the end of the form. The sequence is I (1-3-6) II (3-1-5-3) V (1-5-△7-3) III (3-1-5-3) – I (6). I've started you with a lead-in to the polychord lick in Exercise. 8-3. Once learned try it other common keys as well like E♭, F and G. Also review the similar example, Fig. 8-43 (Chap 8) which uses VII triad.

Exercise 8-3

This line is very idiosyncratic Jimmy so once learned, you may want to avoid playing it verbatim and take pieces of it or construct a similar phrase. Here's an example of a "Raney influenced" weaving line for B♭ rhythm changes. Let your imagination roam!

Exercise 8-4

Jimmy's **minor** scale phrases discussed had these characteristics:

- Motion from the 7th (∆7-♮7-6) or 5th (5th-♯5-6)
- Polyrhythmic application (for ex. 123421 in 6/8)
- Sequence
    - Ascending minor 3rds
    - ½ steps up or down.
    - Up a flatted 5th
- Interwoven arpeggios or 3rds (for ex. 1234575)
- Upward motion towards
    - Lower neighbor or ascending melodic minor (56∆7 1)
    - Direct motion from 5th below (5123)

Take a tune written in a minor key, minor blues or with minor chords of long duration (for example a tune with ii-iv motion) and apply these concepts. I've started you with the below examples (ex 8-5, 8-6).

Exercise 8-5 (Scalar with leap and maj7)

Exercise 8-6 (Sequential minors in 6/8)

Exercise 8-7 (Minor with Dorian and minor moving 7th)

Dominant chords and the amount of detail, contrast, and variation applied perhaps distinguishes great jazz artists like Jimmy from others and is evidenced by the 10 pages devoted to it this chapter. See below examples to start you off and apply them to some of your favorite standards. Be sure to insert these ideas contextually and sensibly so that they sound natural and not "stitched in" (another favorite Raney aphorism).

Exercise 8-8 (ii-V7 with ♭9♯9 combo)

Exercise 8-9 (bvi-bII7 substitute)

Exercise 8-10 ("Kessel" variant)

Exercise 8-11 (VI U.S. triad over V7)

Exercise 8-12 (I°△7 sub over V7)

CHAPTER 9: COMPOSITIONAL, DEVELOPMENT AND PHRASING CONCEPTS

We've talked a lot about Jimmy's phrasing and rhythmic devices. But much of the discussion of it has been in isolation. This chapter will really focus in on the compositional process and how rhythm and other techniques are applied in solo development.

A. DIMINUTION

Jimmy sometimes used a technique called diminution to propel the time forward and create anticipation and melodic interest. Diminution is a compositional process of gradually contracting note values to smaller ones, which all come together to coincide with the finish of the phrase. See in Fig. 9-1 over his composition, "Chewish Chive and English Brick" (2nd chorus, bars 15-18) how the note values decrease from half notes to dotted quarters to eighths creating a typical jazz drum pattern:

Fig. 9-1[135]

Melodically it's clear what he is doing: the melody rises in half steps and connects the 3rd of F to the 3rd of B♭-. A natural dramatic accent is created by the leap to the 9th C and then motion down in steps to the root of the dominant chord E♭7. If you sing through the phrase, it becomes very clear how melody and rhythm converge on the E♭.

A similar process is used on his live solo to Just Friends (after the 8th note scale on A♭-7). Singing through the phrases just rhythmically makes it clear how the phrase is "pulled into" the ending note on F. But couple that with clear harmonic motion and cadence from A7 to D-, you begin to see that inevitability in Jimmy's phrasing —where all things seem to come together in musical confluence and "rightness."

Fig. 9-2 [136]

Fig. 9-3 is another example of the process, where short phrases are brought closer and closer together in an imitative process with a finalizing shorter note phrase. Again, much of the cohesion is handled purely rhythmically, but with the descending neighbor tone motive the phrase's melodic and harmonic target become very clear.

---

135. Raney, *Raney '81*
136. Raney/Collins, *Actors Theatre*

Fig. 9-3 ("What is This Thing Called Love" solo, bars 1-6) [137]

B. SET-UP PHRASES

Jimmy also uses a process where simpler, melodic (yet rhythmically energizing) turns of phrase in longer note values are used to contrast with and set up complex active eighth note passages that follow them. Although the process can include sequential development (and often does as in Figs. 9-4 -9-6) set-up phrases don't have to possess an abundance of related melodic materials as much as the right contrast in energy and rhythm. The method differs with the one discussed in chapter 2, where continuous lines were made more interesting with the introduction of interesting accents and rhythms. Set-up passages are especially effective in faster tempos because it keeps the listener in active anticipation and the solo in proper balance.

Fig. 9-4 shows a simple but effective setup phrase used after the two-bar break on "Cross Your Heart." What is effective about it is the rhythmic push coupled with the almost conversational #4-5-1 question/answer pair. Fig. 9-5 shows the basic rhythmic underpinning of the phrase.

Fig. 9-4 ("Cross Your Heart," solo break)[138]

Fig. 9-5

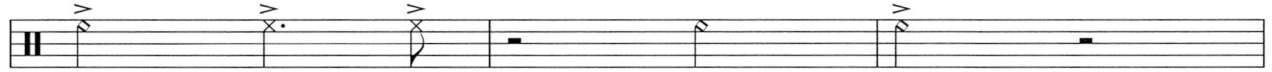

After this simple set-up, two groups of faster eighth notes are played. The first is quick and the second is longer as it continues deftly thru a harmonically complex turnaround.

---

137. Raney, *Raney '81*
138. Raney, *Quartet '55*

Fig. 9-6[139]

A very similar style phrase and process is used on a short one chorus solo on a 1951 Music Minus One album. It uses the same lower neighbor interval idea, quarters (with astute eighth pushes) and sequential development, although much more elaborate in this latter aspect than the previous example (The melodic content of the opening sequence will be analyzed in a later section).

What Jimmy is clearly doing here is "cooking the rhythm" by developing short melodic phrases that build anticipation both melodically and rhythmically. The five beats of space in measure 4 to 5 is just as thrilling as when he finally delivers the faster phrases in bars 6-11 and his trademark b5 bend. This one still knocks me out every time hear it!

Fig. 9-7 [140]

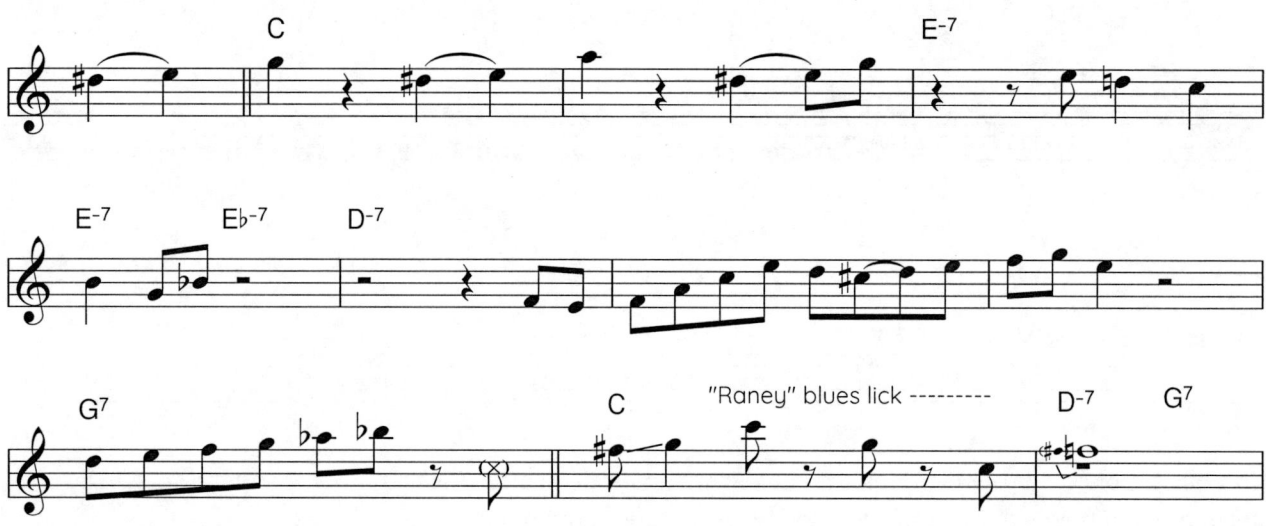

He uses a similar phrase in the same key on his solo to Brookmeyer's "No Male for Me." Jimmy really cooks the rhythm again on this but pushes the beat even more with a strongly accented 4th beat. The strong drum rhythm suggested by the passage is shown in Fig. 9-9:

---

139. Ibid
140. Jimmy Raney, *Music Minus One Guitar,* MMO, 1951

Fig. 9-8 (bars 17-20)[141]

Fig. 9-9

And finally, the full phrase realization after the set-up is shown in rig 9-10. Note how the eighth notes just fly out after the set-up phrase. It's like setting up a great fastball with a curveball!

Fig. 9-10[142]

The set-up passage for Fig. 9-12 is an elongated variant of this common minor scale phrase in Fig. 9-11:

Fig. 9-11

Fig. 9-12 shows how the minor scale phrase is used to set-up faster phrases on his sprightly "Jim's Tune." There is some imitation between bars 10-12 and 13-14 in both the quarter-eighth rhythm and the 9-8 suspensions on the relative harmony (B♭- and E♭-). But the imitation is stopped at bar 15 to launch the eighth note run. This is further enhanced by the pause on G♭7, adding more anticipation.

---

141. Raney, *Brookmeyer*
142. Ibid.

Fig. 9-12 ("Jim's Tune" solo, bars 9-16) [143]

A similar process is used in Fig. 9-13. There are 2 imitative phrases in larger note values to set up the quicker eighth note line. Note also the 6/4 implication in the set-up, the contrasting triadic E♭ material and the bridging material in bars 11-12. The A♭- scale line is prepared by the A-7 and G- fragments prior and imitates their beat placement on 2 to tie everything together.

Fig. 9-13 ("The Flag is Up" solo) [144]

The rhythmically driving set up in Fig. 9-13 is used several times in the solo quoted previously ("Jim's Tune"). There is (for lack of better words) an almost "slingshot" analogy to this process where energy is built up in the long notes and released in the quicker notes (like the potential-kinetic energy relationship). The device of alternation between **energy building** phrases and **energy releasing** phrases is masterful and for that the 16 bars are presented in their entirety (see Fig. 9-14).

---

143. Raney, *Brookmeyer*
144. Ibid.

Fig. 9-14 ("Jim's Tune" solo, bars 24-41) [145]

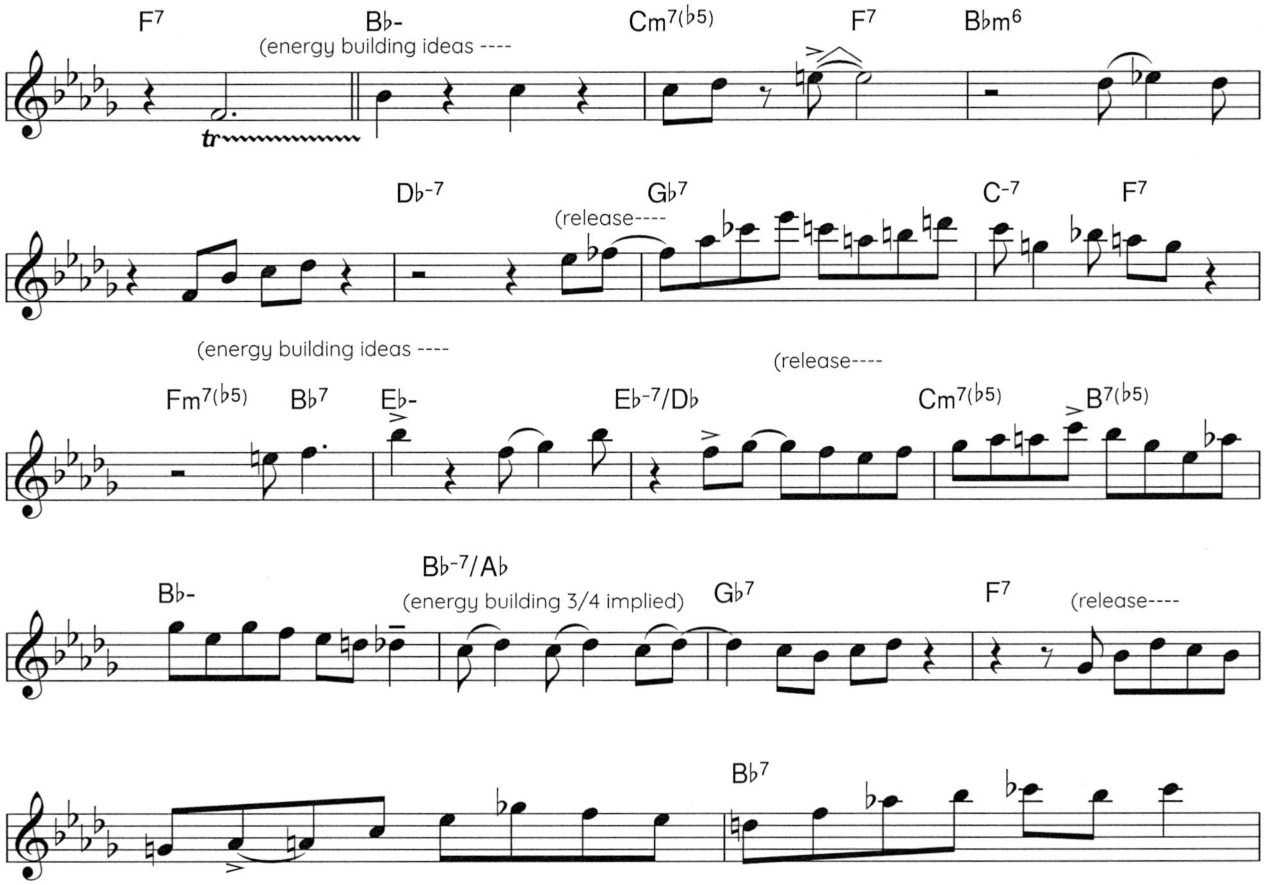

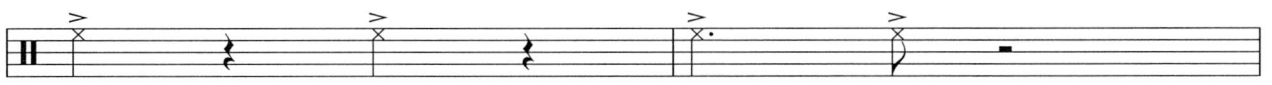

How are the passages I've indicated exactly "energy building"? In a word: rhythmically. It starts with the trill in pick-up measure 24 which is natural energy-building device (it's initiated in response to the drummer's snare drum roll). At the rhythmic core of Bars 25-26 is actually a pretty common quarter-quarter dotted quarter hit pattern. Jimmy enhances the momentum by playing a blues bend on the 4th note.

Fig. 9-15 The rhythmic patterns underlying bars 25-26, 32-34, 37-38:

Bars 25-26:

---

145. Ibid.

CHAPTER 9 COMPOSITIONAL, DEVELOPMENT AND PHRASING CONCEPTS B. SETUP PHRASES

In bars 32-34 a similar rhythmic pattern (with extra dotted quarter) is played transposed:

Bars 32-34:

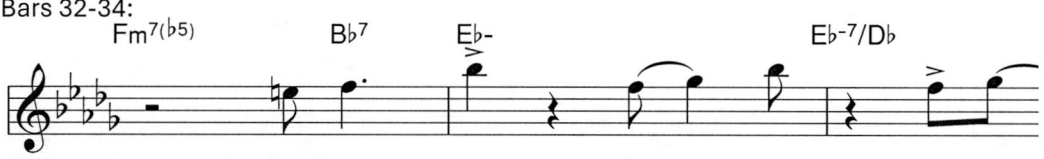

Bars 37-38 clearly imply a 3-2 clave rhythm:

Bars 37-38

C. ASYMMETRICAL JOINS

Jimmy has a knack for joining phrases together asymmetrically on unexpected beats, creating strong counter-rhythms against 4/4. He often splices an arpeggio or phase on a weak beat before the previous phrase is finished. Or sometimes he adds extra notes, displacing the line. Or he reverses that procedure by starting a phrase that would displace if started on strong beat and moving it to a weak beat so that it resolves to beat one.

The general idea is *to challenge yourself rhythmically*. If you are running eighths and find yourself accenting strong beats too much (like Fig. 9-16), then you are probably not doing everything you could to create an interesting line. Figs. 9-16 and 9-17 shows how a simple "add/subtract" procedure (discussed Chap. 6) can make a big difference in line interest. The line goes from a 4+4+4+4 eighth note grouping to 6+4+6.

Fig. 9-16 ("straight" line pattern)

Fig. 9-17 ("rhythmically enhanced" line pattern. A and A♯ added, C and B♭ subtracted)

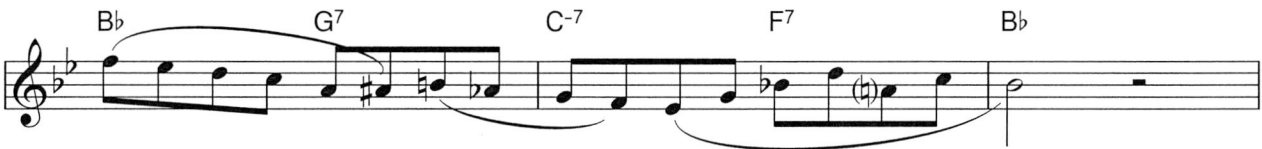

One of his favorite techniques is to start with a II-V lick then slur right into another arpeggio. In Fig. 9-18, the sudden slurring of the second F♯ note makes the initial phrase feel like 7/8. Also note how he doesn't start the II-V on the downbeat but rather anticipates it on beat 4.

Fig. 9-18 ("Anthropology" solo, bars 17-19)[146]

A similar example is shown in Fig. 9-19. Although the phrase initially starts on beat 1, there is similarity in the initial feeling of 7/8, the shape of the line and a consistent anticipation of the downbeat in each phrase piece:

Fig. 9-19 ("Stella By Starlight," Live in Tokyo, 1976, bars 14-18)

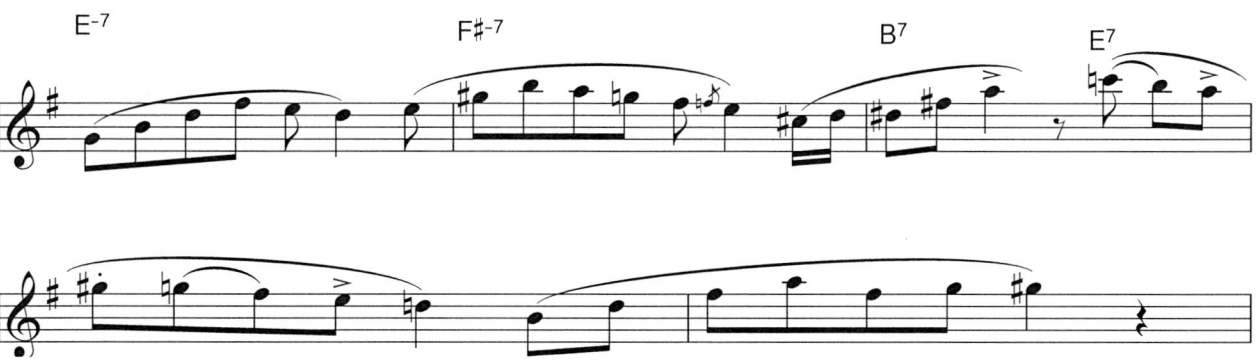

In Fig. 9-20, the II-V pattern starts on beat 3. The asymmetrical join is created by the pairing of the B♭maj9 arpeggio with the II –V on the "and" of 3 (bar 10). This gives the effect of grouping the eighths in 9+7 as the phrase re-grounds on the F- scale on the 3rd beat of bar 11.

---

146. Raney, *Live in Tokyo*

Fig. 9-20 ("What is This Thing Called Love" solo, bars 9-11)[147]

The next example, Jimmy makes an asymmetrical cross-cutting arpeggio on D-△, but it comes after the beat (1+). Given the beginning of the phrase on the 4+ there is a 5/4 implication there (see Fig. 9-21).

Fig. 9-21 ("Just Friends" solo, 3rd chorus, bars 11-13) [148]

The previous asymmetrical join examples were essentially slurring from below on upwards arpeggios to cut across the time. Jimmy would also achieve this effect by a sudden leap and then downwards figures against the time. He liked to do this with trademark multiple neighbor tones which were often preceded by a leap of a 7th as in Fig. 9-22:

Fig. 9-22 ("Anthropology" solo, 3rd chorus, bars 26-29)[149]

Raney N.T. lick back to back - 5 beats apart

Note again how a strong unexpected asymmetrical phrase against the time leads to metrical superimpositions. 5/4-time implication comes about because of the 5 beats separating the two neighbor tone phrases. We talked about this metric aspect of this neighbor tone pattern in the previous section (Fig. 8-32).

Jimmy is found of pairing enclosure sequences with inverted arpeggios as noted in the inverted arpeggios section (Fig. 8-14). But he usually does so asymmetrically, often overlapping the enclosure across the bar line and beginning the inverted arpeggio on another beat.

Fig. 9-23 is a good example of this, effectively mixing and matching enclosures, inverted arpeggios, and other elements asymmetrically, traversing 5 bars rather naturally. This example is more typical of his later playing where lines keep going without a break, naturally accenting the phrase shapes to create clear structures within that long run of eighths. (In the example, arp=arpeggio, encl=enclosure, inv. arp=inverted arpeggio.)

---

147. Raney, *Raney '81*
148. Raney/Collins, *Actors Theatre*
149. Raney, *Live in Tokyo*

Fig. 9-23 ("Anthropology" solo, 2nd chorus, bars 26-32) [150]

Fig. 9-24 is an even more extreme example of asymmetric lines without pause (nearly the entire 12 bars), using mixed 6/8 and 4/8 polyrhythmic scales and integrated phrases. His continuous line playing style is usually more characteristic in faster tunes rather than this medium tempo blues example. However, the passage is very much in the spirit of the teachings of Chapter 2 that uses mixed scale group accents to create line interest purely by accents (Figs. 2-5, 2-6 for ex.). Generally, every leap after a downward scale is accented and marks a beginning of a phrase group.

Fig. 9-24 ("Billie's Bounce" solo, 6th chorus, bars 2-12)[151]

---

150. Ibid.
151. Jimmy Raney In Nashville, Private Collection, 1984

CHAPTER 9A-C EXERCISES: DIMINUTION, SET UPS, AND ASYMMETRICAL JOINS

Let's begin to apply what we have learned in this section. Exercise 9-1 deals with the concept of diminution discussed at the beginning of this chapter. The realization is over the changes to "It's You Or No One" using contracting rhythmic values from half notes, dotted quarters, quarters to eighths (it is not necessary to be absolutely strict in the diminution). Try your own study on the tune "All the Things You Are" (Ex. 9-2) or another jazz tune you are very familiar with. The idea is to create a coherent phrase where everything "comes together" logically and musically — the notes, rhythm, and the harmony.

Exercise 9-1 Diminution Concept (Solo over changes to "It's You Or No One")

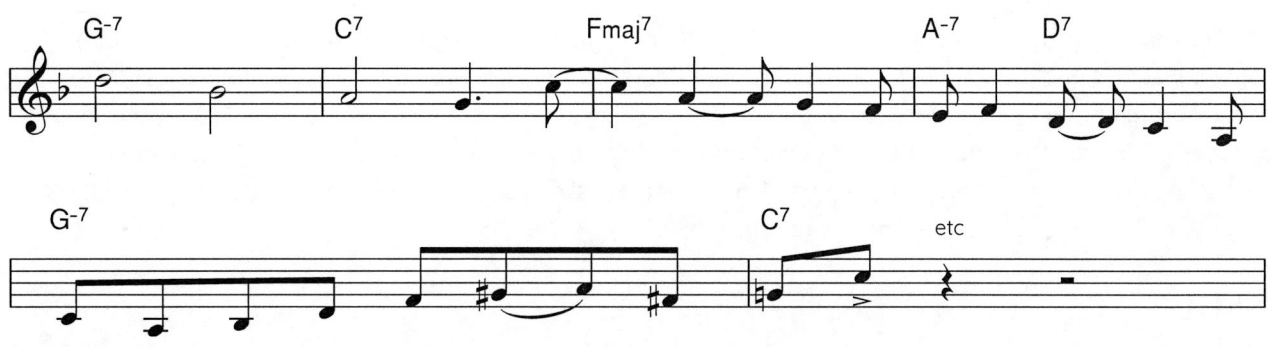

Exercise 9-2 Diminution Concept (Solo over changes to "All the Things You Are")

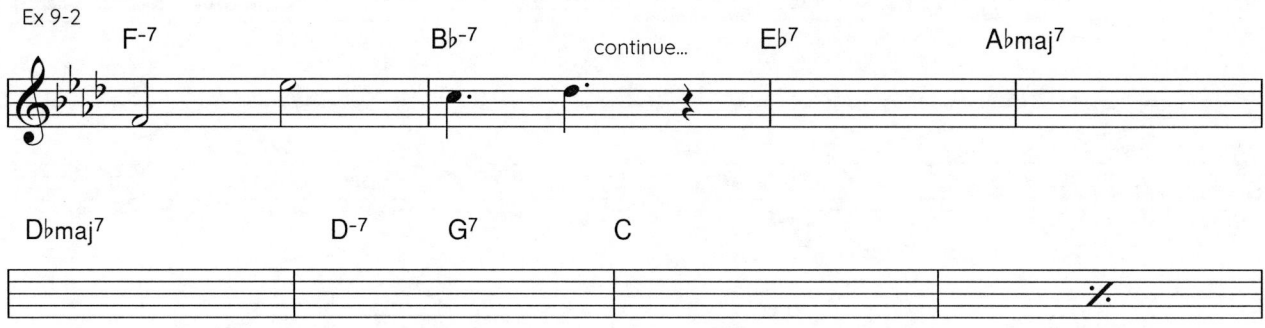

Earlier in the chapter in section B, Jimmy's concept of *set-up phrases* was covered, where long notes in rhythmically driving patterns create anticipation for faster eighth passages and heighten their impact. As mentioned, it has a similar developmental goal as diminution. Exercise 9-3 is a sample of the process over "I'll Remember April." Set-up phrases are used in bars 1-2, 5-6 and 15-16. In addition to the set-up phrases, the sample features several Raney influenced licks. See if you can pick them out.

Exercise 9-3 Set-up phrase realization (Solo over changes to "I'll Remember April")

Continue the set-up phrases shown in exercises 9-4 to 9-6:

Exercise 9-4 "Have You Met Miss Jones"

Exercise 9-5 "Just One of Those Things"

Exercise 9-6 "My Secret Love"

Earlier this chapter we covered "asymmetrical joins." Part of coming up with interesting line joins is understanding the rhythmic implication of your potential pieces. Here are some common Raney line components defined rhythmically that you can use to start. Continue the phrase logically. Follow-up changes are up to you.

CHAPTER 9 COMPOSITIONAL CONCEPTS: CHAPTER 9A-C EXERCISES

Exercise 9-7

Exercise 9-8

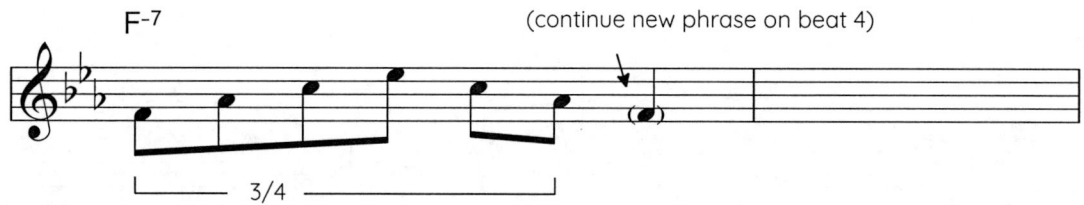

Exercise 9-9

Exercise 9-10

Ex. 9-11 shows a sample asymmetric line over the beginning changes to "Woody n' You" in Jimmy's style. Note the beat 2 start, the typical II-V lick and the 3/4 over 4/4 feeling created by overlapping phrases. Continue the next four bars and the remainder of the solo. Look to create familiar bebop phrase structures but with an asymmetrical approach that makes the time "pop". Thinking in polyrhythms (as noted in Chap 2) can be helpful in achieving this.

Exercise 9-11 "Woody 'n You"

D. "EVOLVING" SEQUENCE & EXPANSION

Many have commented there is inevitability in Jimmy's lines; they always seem to end up where there are supposed to. Part of that is his mastery of sequence in his lines but not obvious sequence schemes, as commented in earlier chapters, given that would probably lead to more commonplace results. There is almost always commonality between phrases but with slight changes made, developing a portion of the previous phrase, and adding to it and then that piece itself is developed upon, until the entire larger phrase is built of these <u>related, evolving pieces</u>. Often the final piece is different from the initial but there is nevertheless a sense of having traveled logically.

Fig. 9-25 shows an example of this type of sequential development. Jimmy takes commonplace materials, in this case harmonic outlines, but with the aid of rhythm, logical phrase lengths and clear melodies, he builds a complete intro statement that leads perfectly to the head melody of the "Song Is You":

Fig. 9-25[152]

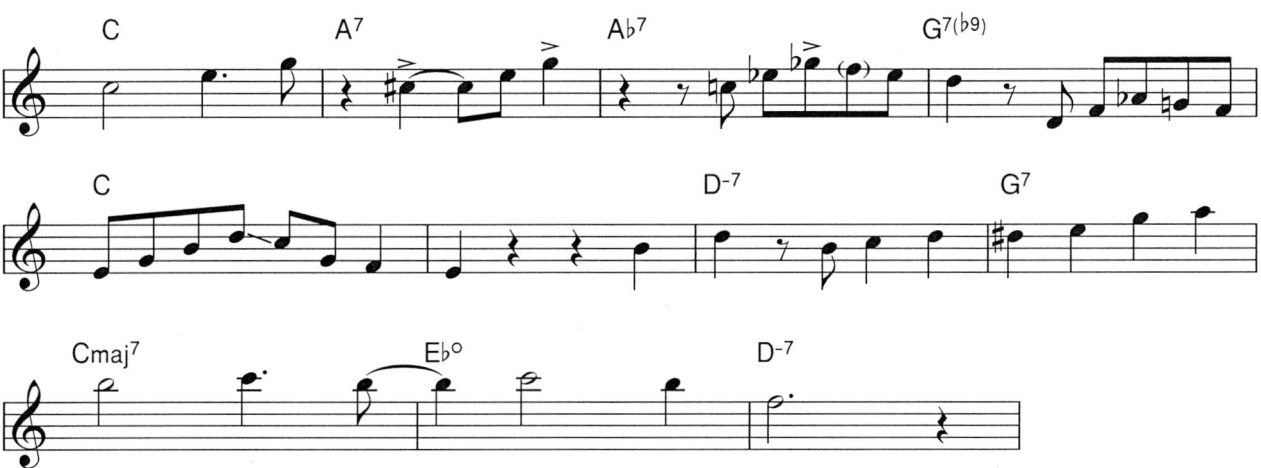

Harmonically this is pretty easy to grasp with triads and 7ths clearly outlined. But the real trick is how each piece is developed from the previous and expanded. Below is an outline:

A. Statement (triad up)

B. Related statement (similar triad, rhythmically altered)

---

152. Raney, *The Master*

C. Answer statement incomplete (similar triad up then scale down to half cadence on D)

D. Answer statement completed and continued (triad up and scale down to imperfect cadence on E)

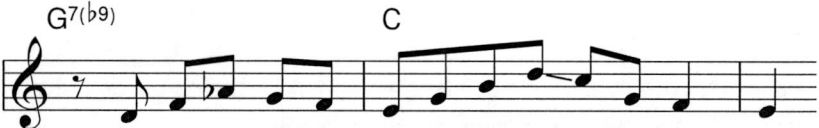

E. There is a final completion of the cadence to C (circled) but it is embedded within a continuation:

In the previous section we talked about diminution but the development scheme here could be viewed as the opposite: *augmentation*. Notice the later start of each phrase in the first 3 bars: beat 1, beat 2 and then a pickup to beat 3:

Also note the increase in phrase lengths:

And after an initial lessening in note duration, an increase in note duration which includes the head melody:

Here's another example that puts the **sequential expansion** idea to work. In Fig. 9-26 an initial syncopated idea on the B-11 chord is imitated rhythmically and transposed, then a secondary motive develops at the tail end of the idea on a repeated note chord outline which in turn is developed, until finally bridging "free" material moves it into double time feel in the bridge. In the diagram, a non-strict imitation adds a number (A, A1, B, B1, etc.) and an expansion uses a +.

Fig. 9-26 ("Darn that Dream" solo, bars 14-17)[153]

There is a sense of expansion in the line and a distinct feeling of acceleration towards the cadence to the bridge modulation; that is made clear from the move from 16ths to 32nds and the increase in chords.

E. THEMATIC CONTRASTS & REPETITION

Let us look at another type of development in a shorter 2 chorus solo, "I Love You" from *The Influence*. Sequence is not as much at play here as in the previous example. This solo's continuity is achieved differently, by **pairing contrasting elements against each other** and using **"purposeful" repetition.**

There is a tonal and rhythmic contrast between the first 4 bars (including the 2-bar break) and the two measures that follow it; the first part contains more dissonant intervals, chromatic harmony and 3/8 rhythm while the second is more tonic harmony (over F major) and is more grounded to the downbeats. Essentially this is a tonal and rhythmic tension-release scheme where the first 6 bars iron out a close interval and traverse thru a chromatic harmony to the tonic.

Fig. 9-27 (intro to bar 2)[154]

Mapping it out you could look at it this way:

---

153. Raney, *Live in Tokyo*
154. Raney, *The Influence*

CHAPTER 9 COMPOSITIONAL, DEVELOPMENT AND PHRASING CONCEPTS E. THEMATIC CONTRASTS AND REPETITION

Fig. 9-28

In addition to a reinstatement of similar material, there is also a feeling for increasing note activity towards a change in section, followed by decreasing note activity. This is another kind of tension-release formula:

Fig. 9-29 (bars 3-6) [155]

Fig. 9-30 (Bars 7-10)

You can see how note activity towards a new section happens in bars 11-15, but the formula needs to be reversed on the F major for notes to slow down on the arriving A major key; the F major is the transition (♭VI pivot) not the point of rest as before. Also note the 3/8 rhythm and "expanding interval" theme from the opening measures is developed in a related way in the key of A, making that a **foreshadowing** of this section. This is a classical compositional technique, where initial motives are redeveloped by imitative material in the new key, creating continuity and an unfolding development.

Fig. 9-31 (Bars 11-15)

And just to keep this idea going there is note activity at the end of the A major to transition back to ii-V in F major harmony:

Fig. 9-32 (Bars 15-19)

---

155. Raney, *The Influence*

In this particular solo there is quite bit of restatement of lines. We noted that in bars 3-10 on the G-7b5 (B♭-) changes. Although somewhat subjective, I believe the reason is in a sense like creating effective oratory. You engage the listener and create drama by **restating the idea pointedly.** He does this here and also creates a 3/4 pattern:

Fig. 9-33 (Bars 26-27)

Likewise, he takes the same approach on these measures.

Fig. 9-34 (Bars 1-2, 2nd chorus with pick-up)

and here as well:

Fig. 9-35 (2nd chorus, bars 19-20)

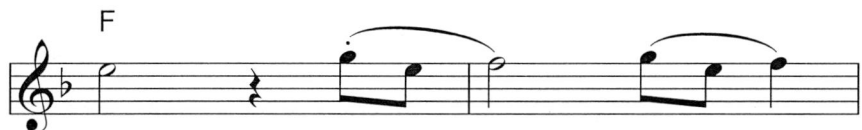

And finally, there is a repetition of similar phrases across choruses.

Fig. 9-36 (Bars 17-20)

Fig. 9-37 (2nd chorus, Bars 17-20)

Fig. 9-38 (Bars 21-24)

Fig. 9-39 (2nd chorus, bars 21-24)

Overall, as we have seen the B♭- minor changes seem to invite more note activity and complexity while the A major and G-7 C7 to F major sections seem to be paced measures with simpler melodic chordal outlines. Interestingly however the high point in terms of note activity and pitch seems to happen near the end of the solo. But given the carefully paced measured prior and the relatively short 2 chorus solo this formula seems inevitable.

Fig. 9-40 (2nd chorus, bars 26-32)

F. THE "UNDERCURRENT OF THREE"

As mentioned, Jimmy's phrases always seem to have an undercurrent of implied polymeter, in particular 3/4 or 6/4. So far, we have quoted more examples from later period playing where these polyrhythmic concepts were perhaps more overt and intentional. But was this approach always present in his playing, even in earlier periods? I think there is a strong case for it. Fig. 9-41 shows the first 16 bars of his solo to his classic "Signal" from his first record in 1953:

Fig. 9-41[156]

Fig. 9-42 shows a re-beaming of the excerpt with reference to implied meter in 3/4. Again, this is based on strong phrase pulls based on chord shapes, jazz clichés and accents.

---

156. Raney, *Jimmy Raney Plays*

Fig. 9-42

To get a feel for these implied meters, I would recommend playing the 3/4 phrases in groups and repeating them several times in a row. Even if the implied polymeter in this passage seems like a stretch to you, strongly accenting these transcribed lines in 3/4 feel against 4/4 is in the spirit of Jimmy's teachings about freedom from overly "straight" playing (and jazz in general) and doing this changes your perception about the limitations of the bar line. Fig. 9-43 lifts out bars 3-4 and 5-6 and arranges them in 3/4 for repeated practice.

Fig. 9-43

If you weren't convinced by the 3/4 undercurrent of the previous examples, perhaps you would be convinced in the next ones, which take place later in the same solo. Here's the first one that includes a Barney Kessel influenced lick in the second bar:

Fig. 9-44

There is a frequent suggestion of 3/4 at various spots in the third chorus of the solo:

Fig. 9-45

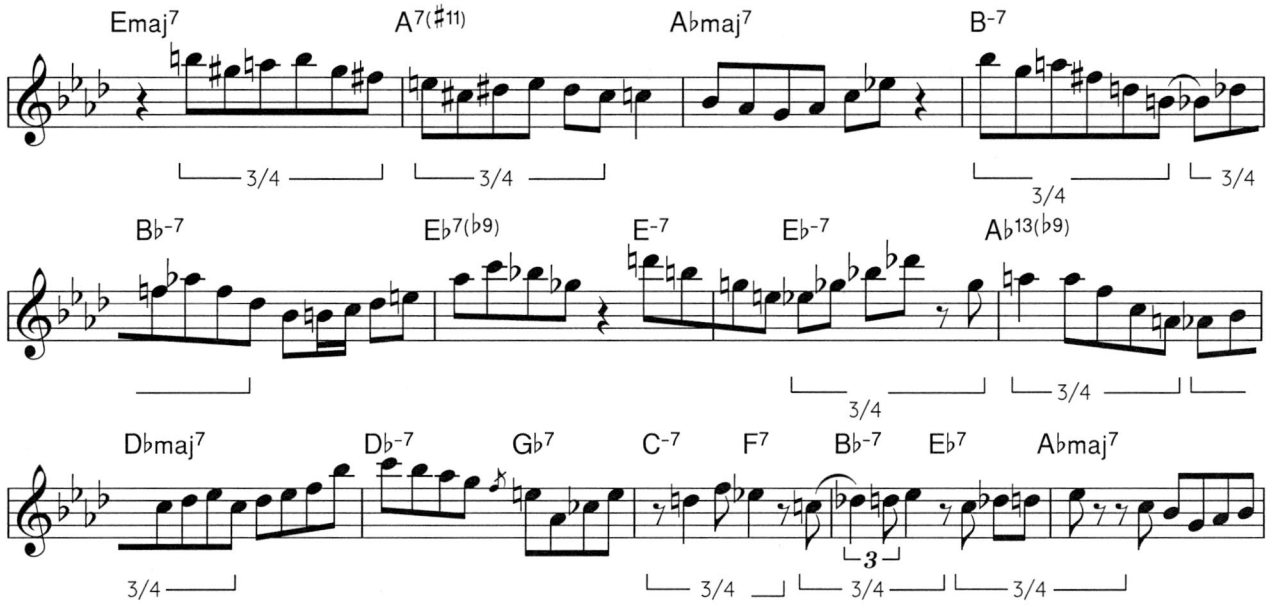

In terms of 6/4, they are two implied references in Fig. 9-45 (bars 2-3, 15-16). But a clear 6/4 repetition occurs in the 4th solo chorus here:

Fig. 9-46

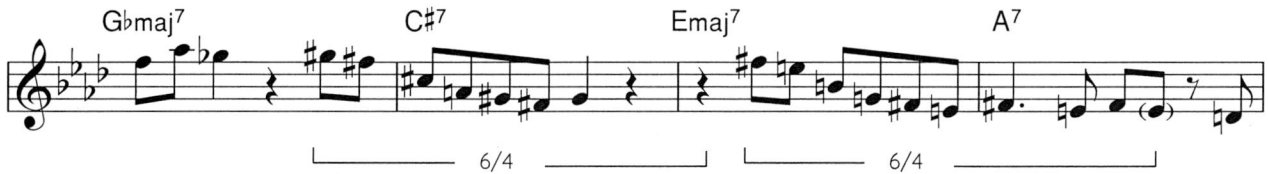

CHAPTER 9D-F EXERCISES:
EVOLVING SEQUENCE, THEMATIC CONTRAST & "UNDERCURRENT OF THREE"

Let's practice some of the concepts discussed in sections D-F. I've started off each exercise for you below. Please follow the specified concept and instructions and add at least a few bars of your own development.

Exercise 9-12 (Evolving Sequence)

("It Could Happen to You")

initial idea   imitative idea with development

Exercise 9-13 (Evolving Sequence)

("Just Friends")

Exercise 9-14 (Thematic Contrast)

("All of You")

Exercise 9-15 ("Purposeful Repetition")

("Our Love is Here to Stay")

Exercise 9-16 ("Undercurrent of Three")

("The Song is You")

Exercise 9-17 ("Undercurrent of Three")

("Donna Lee")

G: QUESTION AND ANSWER

There is a conversational quality in Jimmy's playing, which seems to pose a question then supply the answer. Another definition of this is "call and response." Fig. 9-47 is a good simple example. It's a reversal of the root direction (♯4-5-1 up, ♯4-5-1 down) and the root up phrase is answered by the root down phrase. Interest is also created because of the asymmetry of the longer question vs. shorter answer.

Fig. 9-47[157]

Fig. 9-48 is a similar lower neighbor idea in quarter notes. It is a classic development format: idea, related idea and final unifying idea containing the original motive and then a continuation. I think this phrase is somewhat influenced by Louis Armstrong's famous vocal scat on "West End Blues."

---

157. Raney, *Brookmeyer*

CHAPTER 9 COMPOSITIONAL, DEVELOPMENT AND PHRASING CONCEPTS G. QUESTION AND ANSWER

Fig. 9-48[158]

Clearly the lower neighbor b5 is a favorite phrase developer for Jimmy. Here again he uses it as a repeated motive at the beginning of "Isn't It Romantic":

Fig. 9-49[159]

Notice though that he doesn't *overdo* it by repeating the Bb-E-F again after bar 3. Instead, he develops a 3rd below (C-Db) in bars 4-5 and then moves down to another part of the scale and blues mode. The rising double note eighths from dominant to tonic (bar 6) and the implied dotted quarter rhythm (bar 7) relates back to bar 1 and ties everything together.

But as usual, this isn't all there is to it. Jimmy is playing these simple call and response phrases with deceptively subtle rhythms. In Fig. 9-49, with the rhythmic transposition of E-F motive in bar 1 to beat 4 (with a pick-up) in bar 2, there is a clear 7/4 implication (plus an oblique reference to Arlen's "Blues in the Night"). The 7/4 is also implicated by the 3rd phrase starting with a pickup to beat 3, bar 4 (14 beats from beginning) and then the rising double noted motive starting on the 2nd beat of bar 6 (21 beats from beginning), Fig. 9-50 shows the 7/4 interpreted grouping of the passage:

Fig. 9-50

---

158. Raney, *MMO Guitar*
159. Raney, *Brookmeyer*

Along similar question-answer development lines is this Raney solo from his 3rd chorus of a 1954 Billie Holiday concert on "Billie's Blues." The first bar blues lick is imitated with added bluesy 3rds in the next bar (and draws a "yeah!" from a bandmate):

Fig. 9-51[160]

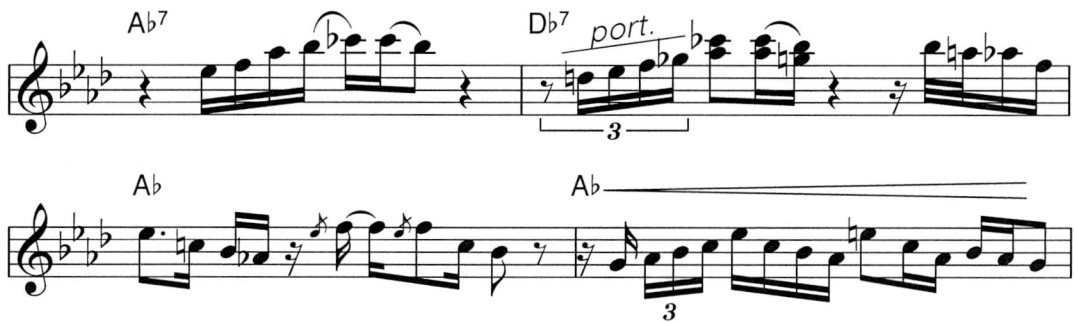

In the bars following the blues licks he develops a highly melodic repeated motive phrase starting on a *downward* A♭ pentatonic (5-3-2-1), varying the top note (5-6 in bar 3, 5th — ♯5 in bar 4) and the rhythm, transitioning to the IV7 chord. Each piece is similar but slightly altered to respond to the previous phrase, and the 4th bar is clearly answering the 3rd bar and completing the overall 2 bar statement begun in bar 3:

Fig. 9-52[161]

These measures also make for a nice compliment to the blues phrase started previously which began on an upward A♭ pentatonic (Fig. 9-51).

The important point to emphasize about call and response imitative *development* in Jimmy's playing is that it's not about taking a simple phrase and repeating it for the sake of recognition. That would be too easy. **It's a compositional process for making a short phrase i**nto a longer phrase and getting the listener to *hear that unfold*. A 2-beat idea becomes a 1 measure idea which becomes a 2-measure idea which becomes a 4-measure idea, and so in.

This is why a *related-but-different* track works towards that end. The listener understands the relatedness of one idea to another, but also senses that *something else* is down the road because of the variation and then anticipates being able to tie all that together *when the rest is heard*. Just like any good story you are listening to for the first time, and Jimmy was a master storyteller.

An additional thing to point out is that this blues passage is another example of diminution and **increase in harmonic rhythm towards a cadence.** The imitation scheme contracts and there is an increase in note speed and implied harmonic rhythm towards bar 5. See Fig. 9-53 to see how this development scheme is mapped out:

---

160. Billie Holiday, *Live at Jazz Club USA,* Cologne, United Artists, 1954
161. Ibid.

CHAPTER 9 COMPOSITIONAL, DEVELOPMENT AND PHRASING CONCEPTS G. QUESTION AND ANSWER

Fig. 9-53

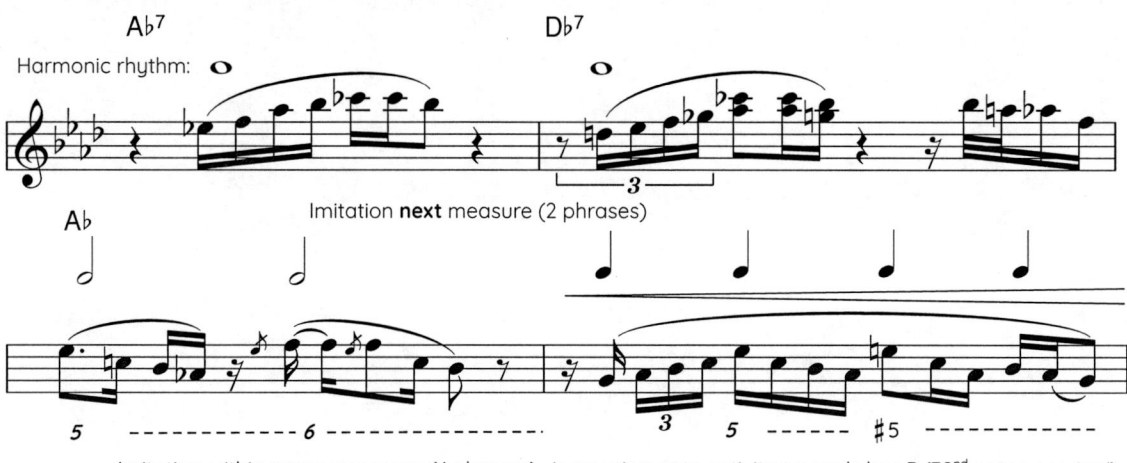

Further, the increase in activity continues in bar 5 (not shown here) where he begins a long run in 32nd notes.

This idea of increase in energy and underlying pulse over choruses on slow blues solos (especially in the transition from bar 4 to 5) is really nothing new. It's just harder to pick-up on bebop's more hybrid, harmonically detailed stylization of the blues.

In the previous examples the question-answer motivic development was pretty easy to pick up on. In Fig. 9-54 it's harder because the motives are somewhat unrelated, but nevertheless it's there because the 2 phrases work so well together.

Fig. 9-54 ("Motion," bars 5-8)[162]

This comes about because the dominant chord phrase is being answered by the tonic phrase and overall, there is clear detailing of the harmonic progression. However, *he avoids an obvious answer by not repeating the exact rhythm* and *shape* like (let's say) the two phrases I created in Fig. 9-55. The second figure is ok, is related and does the job of answering, but it's uninteresting.

Fig. 9-55[163]

So, if I were to come up with one mantra for Jimmy's developmental modus operandi, it would be the *related, but different* technique discussed thus far. This also harkens back to the philosophy behind Jimmy's concepts in Chapter 3 about not making sequences too obvious.

---

162. Raney, *Jimmy Raney Plays*
163. Ibid.

A good example of this sequential development scheme is near the end of the first chorus of Jimmy's solo to "Motion." You can see how he takes the initial motive, an upward B♭ scale combined with a downward arpeggio on E-7b5, repeats this motion while resolving to the dominant A7 harmony, and then changes up the upward scale motion with a neighbor tone and downward 7th arpeggio on the D major. Again, there is that idea, related idea, finalizing unifying idea scheme referred to Fig. 9-30. There is also clear development of essential (IIØ-V7-I) as well as extended harmony (13, ♭9, ♯11, 7-6).

Fig. 9-56 ("Motion" solo, bars 25-27) [164]

Here's another example of "related but different" development in the beginning of "Signal." It uses upper scale fragment motives modulating downwards over changing chords.

Fig. 9-57 ("Signal" solo, bars 1-6) [165]

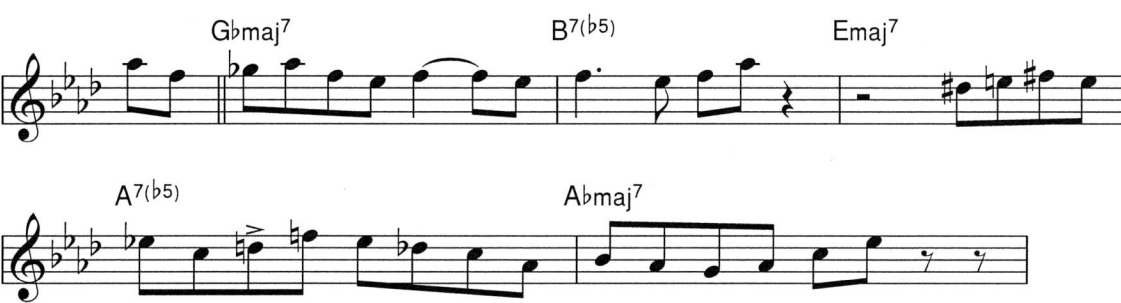

Some of this may be hard to pick up on. Let me lay out the commonalities for you:

- Scale motive 1 (pickup to bar 1):

- Related scale motive 2 (bars 3-4, permutated)

- Related scale motive 3 (bar 4)

---

164. Raney, *Jimmy Raney Plays*
165. Ibid.

- Finishing phrase with upward 3rd (bar 2)

- Related finishing phrase with upward 3rd (bar 5)

The trick is seeing the relatedness of bar 5's finishing phrase with bar 2's finishing phrase (focus on the upward 3rd that finishes each). You then begin to see how the passage is in 3 parts and bars 3-4 relate and bridge bars 1-2 and bars 5-6.

H: "DRAWING THE HARMONY"

Still another aspect of the continuity of Jimmy's style emphasizes notes revealing the harmonic motion. These tones serve to pull in the lines to a specific target – in essence, **drawing the harmony in single lines.** Here are two examples of this from the same solo. The first is actually a re-quote of the head melody but it does serve to demonstrate a working concept reflected in both his compositions and solos:

Fig. 9-58 ("Motion," bars 28-30)[166]

The above passage is an example of "hidden counter-melody." To see it, look at the excerpt in Fig. 9-46 with the stems reversed showing 2 melodies. Notice how they come together, the lower melody moving up and the upper melody moving down, eventually converging on the C#:

Fig. 9-59

A similar counter-melody thing happens later in the solo:

---

166. Raney, *Jimmy Raney Plays*

Fig. 9-60 ("Motion" solo, bars 25-27)

The top melody portion is moving down from C-B♭-A-G-F♯ (see circled notes in Fig. 9-61) while the lower part anchors the harmony a 6th below.

Fig. 9-61[167]

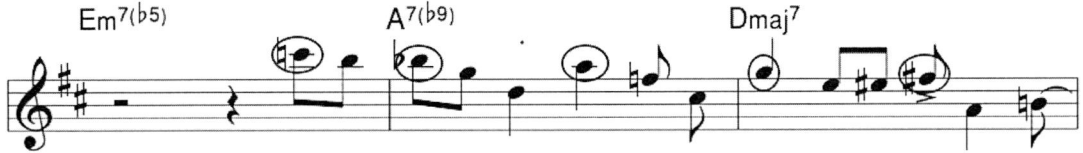

Fig. 9-62 ("Isn't It Romantic" solo, bars 8-9)[168]

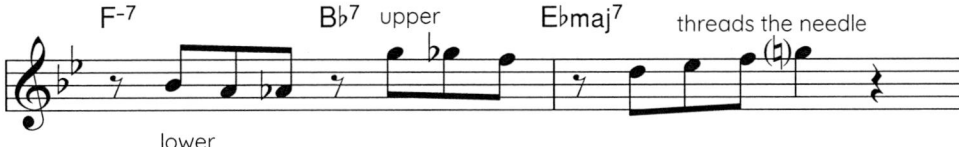

This example was used in an earlier chapter about sequence, but it is relevant to the current section in terms of spelling out the harmony. You can see how the essential "expanding interval" thematic concept serves to again **frame the changing harmony thru the measures: E♭7, Gmaj7 and E7#9:**

Fig. 3-10 ("Nowhere," bars 18-23, *JA Vol 20*)

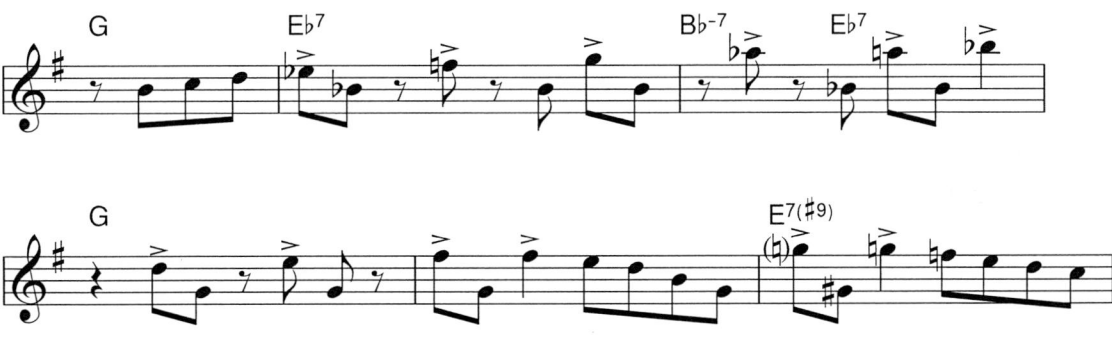

---

167. Ibid.
168. Raney, *Brookmeyer*

CHAPTER 9 COMPOSITIONAL, DEVELOPMENT AND PHRASING CONCEPTS

I: DE-EMPHASIZING BEAT 1

Jimmy has a penchant for weak beat starts and they can be downright surprising when you analyze them (see Fig. 6-10, chapter 6 for example) and he uses similar phrases on different beats. This is another viewpoint on a frequent earlier chapter concept, *harmonic dislocation* (aka displacement).

Beat 4 placement

Many players start on the 4th beat but do so either as a downbeat anticipation or a pick-up to it. While Jimmy does this too, he often starts on 4 and phrases across the bar line, so you find yourself re-queuing the recording to make sure you heard it right. And often this beat early anticipation of the bar line goes with Jimmy's notable skill in phrasing in 5/4.

The "Signal" solo from 1953 quoted previously does this. The A♭ and F neighbor tones to G♭ are embedded within a common scalar jazz phrase that normally occurs on the downbeat (see Fig. 9-63).

Fig. 9-63[169]

Fig. 9-64 shows its actual beat placement in the solo and why A♭–F neighbor tones don't feel like pick-ups to beat 1.

Fig. 9-64

He applies this same beat principle on a similar scale phrase on the "Best Thing for You." Note though that the scale relationship is different —from the 5th of the chord rather than the 9th as in Fig. 9-64:

Fig. 9-65 ("Best Thing for You" solo, bars 29-30)[170]

In another early period solo, he begins his solo break on beat 4 rather than beat 1:

---

169. Raney, *Jimmy Raney Plays*
170. Norvo, *Trio '53*

Fig. 9-66 ("On the Square," solo break)[171]

As usual, I can't resist pointing out the **polymetric implications** of this weak beat start. 5/8 rhythm comes about because of Jimmy's *signature 5 note cross-cutting N.T. lick* (on C♯) being paired with the 5 note F-7 lick, followed by the B♭+ broken chord in 3/8 on the downbeat. As mentioned earlier, polymeter is Jimmy's intuitive way of solving displacement. In this case, the beat 4 start is resolved by 5/4. (see Fig. 9-54)

Fig. 9-67

Here are three more instances of attacked 4th beats within the same solo. They are all 1 bar II-Vs phrases that anticipate the downbeat on beat 4, where the II minor idea is 3 beats long and resolves normally beat-wise on the 3rd of the V7 chord on beat 3. Fig. 9-70 uses Jimmy's favorite Io (or ♯ii°) substitute for V7, but the principle is the same rhythmically.

Fig. 9-68 ("Momentum "solo, 4th chorus, bars 5-7)[172]

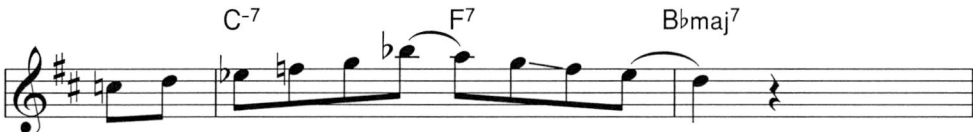

Fig. 9-69 (4th chorus, bars 23-24)[173]

---

171. Raney, *Quartet '54*
172. Raney, *Momentum*
173. Ibid.

Fig. 9-70 (5th chorus, bars 5-7) [174]

Fig. 9-71 is similar to Fig. 9-67 in that it's a 2 bar II-V-I, starts on beat 4 and asymmetrically distributes the V7 portion of the II-V. It starts with a typical 3 beat IIm7 lick, but then the V7 chord extends from beat 3 for 6 beats and defines two different dominant colors, A9 and A13♭9:

Fig. 9-71 ("Pennies from Heaven" solo, 3rd chorus, bars 15-16)[175]

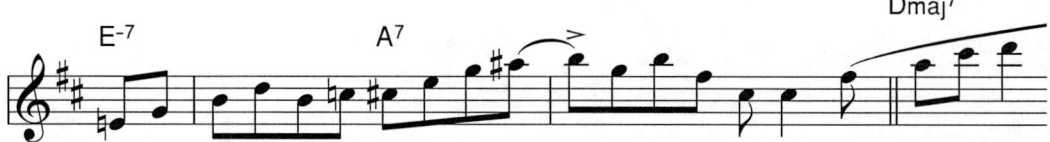

Beat 3 placement

In his second run thru of his classic "Motion" in 1974 (renamed "Momentum" at that time for legal purposes), long lines and fluid beat placement are the bedrock of Jimmy's approach. Because of this, beat 3 starts are common in the solo, phrasing from the middle of the bar. Sometimes this is a 6/4 concept. Other times he continues to displace 4/4 and strongly phrase from beat 3. Fig. 9-72 (bars 4-8), shows an example where he does both.

Fig. 9-72[176]

Just to make the point clear, the C minor change is anticipated by 2 beats and the two 4/4 phrases are followed by a 6-beat phrase, which leaves 4 beats of rest to complete the 8-measure unit. Fig. 9-73 shows how Jimmy is thinking about the location of the harmony and implied phrase lengths on the previous figure:

Fig. 9-73

---

174. Raney, *Momentum*
175. Raney, *Visits Paris, Vol. 1*
176. Raney, *Momentum*

Later in the solo, Jimmy again starts on beat 3, but this time the phrase is delayed two beats:

Fig. 9-74 ("Momentum" solo 3rd chorus, bars 23-27)[177]

From a linear perspective, Jimmy phrased the solo passage in Fig. 9-74 more or less continuously, without overtly accented cross rhythms. However, from a harmonic perspective, Jimmy's lines clearly spell out the location of the changes – and they are not quite on beats 1 and 3. One key to this technique is his signature ♭9♯9 combo phrase discussed in chapter 8 (see circled notes, Fig. 9-75). *The phrase is a 3/4 construction by nature* (like many of his minor II licks) and **its use twice astutely reconciles the phrase's initial 2-beat delay.**

Fig. 9-75

Fig. 9-76 (bars 21-29)[178]

In this section of the solo, he is playing two measure phrases from the middle of the bar until the final little bluesy **3/8 figure played 4 times to bring the line back to one.**

---

177. Ibid.
178. Ibid.

Beat 2 placement

Jimmy often enters on beat 2 with a 3/4 starting phrase, but it's usually part of a bigger sequence, for example the "Another You" excerpt in Fig. 9-77 demonstrates the augmentation method discussed earlier, **where each phrase increases in length:**

Fig. 9-77 ("There Will Never Be Another You" solo, bars 12-15)[179]

---

179. Raney, *The Influence*

CHAPTER 9G-I EXERCISES:
QUESTION/ANSWER, HARMONIC DRAWING, WEAK BEAT EMPHASIS

Exercise 9-18 (Question & Answer)

("Have You Met Miss Jones")

Exercise 9-19 (Question & Answer)

("F minor Blues")

Exercise 9-20 ("Drawing" the Harmony)

("Like Someone in Love")

Exercise 9-21 ("Drawing" the Harmony)

("Green Dolphin Street")

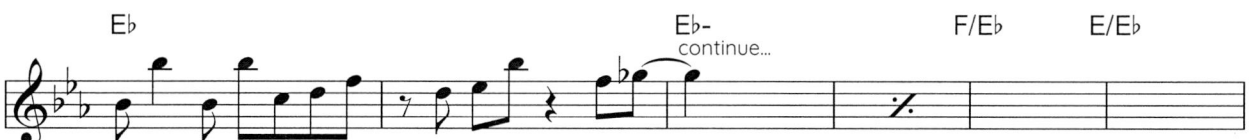

Exercise 9-22 (Weak Beat Emphasis)

("Cherokee")

CHAPTER 10: THE RANEY APPROACH — CREATING A COMPLETE SOLO

We've covered quite a bit of ground in the last two chapters of typical Raney techniques. Now comes the hard part: **to utilize all the techniques discussed together to build a complete and coherent solo**; a difficult proposition given solo coherency and completeness can be a struggle for any student of the art of jazz improvisation. However, the best way to solve this issue is to simply jump and do it and keep making improvements, as is suggested in Jimmy's opening chapters on incrementally improving line.

In preparation for these exercises, let's review a cross section of the important things we've covered so far.

Jimmy's key phrases:

- A. The II-V licks.
- B. The Inverted arpeggio
- C. The multiple neighbor tone lick
- D. The ♭9♯9 V7 (suspensions) phrase
- E. The ♭5 blues lick

Jimmy's favorite harmonic tricks

- F. ♭VIm7 –♭II7 sub for V7
- G. Upper Structure harmony: V13♭9 (VI/V); V7♭9♭5(♭V/V)
- H. I°7 (♭III°) sub for V7
- I. Embellished Major (♯11, ♯5)

Jimmy's favorite phrasing approaches

- J. The "undercurrent of three"/polyrhythm
- K. Evolving sequence
- L. Diminution
- M. Asymmetrical joins
- N. Weak beat starts/displacement.
- O. Harmonic dislocation
- P. Hidden countermelody

Let's approach the problem in **two steps**. In the first exercise we will make a solo that includes key phrases in Jimmy's vocabulary — in essence constructing a solo that *sounds like him* by incorporating his typical lines. This helps confirm your literal absorption of the materials presented to you thus far.

In the second step we are going to try to use his concepts for a solo *without* so much of the phrase thievery. I think this approach echoes the process of assimilating and absorbing the style of a master player: you emulate *literally* first, then *conceptually*. The latter process is more challenging because it asks more of your own conception while at the same time trying to have the player's best practices rub off on you. I have purposely chosen songs that Jimmy has never recorded. I think this helps conceive of Raney ideas *as if you were Jimmy* approaching the tune for the first time. Key concepts are labeled where they occur with its associated letter from the outline on the previous page.

Exercise 10-1 over "The Lady is a Tramp" contains several recognizable Raney clichés. Continue the process thru the bridge (review previous chapter materials if necessary). When continuing the solo, see if you include some of the phrase concepts that I didn't manage to get in it; however, don't force it — be musical and try to make the whole thing hang together stylistically. If you feel boxed in, you may also elect to start your own solo from scratch on the same or different tunes you are familiar with.

Exercise 10-1   Jimmy Raney style solo on "The Lady is a Tramp" in C (first 32 bars)

CHAPTER 10 THE RANEY APPROACH — CREATING A COMPLETE SOLO

In Ex. 10-2, I have purposely tried to avoid literal Raney clichés while still maintaining some of the key concepts. I also tried to integrate phrases that have similarities to those of recent artists. Continue the 2nd chorus of solo as seamlessly as you can or start your own solo from scratch using the same principles.

I personally found this process interesting because it confirmed my belief that Jimmy's early innovations in modernizing jazz guitar have a great deal of relevance to later styles. If you doubt this, I remind you of Fig. 8-44 played 7 decades ago. *Note. I have taken a few liberties with harmonies here and there.

Exercise 10-2 Jimmy Raney "influenced" contemporary solo on the changes of "Star Eyes" in E♭ (1st chorus)

CHAPTER 11: ADDITIONAL SOLO STUDIES & EXERCISES

Picking, Phrasing & The Jazz Eighth Note

THE UNDERLYING PULSE IS THE WEAK 8TH NOTES – THE "ANDS" (AND 3 AND 4 AND ETC)
THESE ARE ACCENTED LIGHTLY, OTHER LARGER GROUPINGS ARE SOMETIMES SUPERIMPOSED ON THESE.

by Jimmy Raney

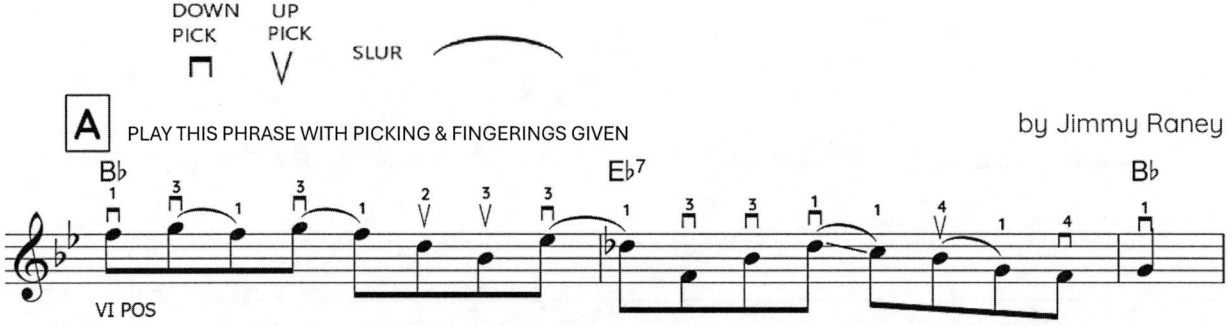

A PLAY THIS PHRASE WITH PICKING & FINGERINGS GIVEN

VI POS

BY USING THE PICKINGS AND FINGERINGS GIVEN, THE NOTE PHRASE & ACCENT THEMSELVES

STILL YOU MUST PRACTICE ACCENTING WITHOUT THE SLURS.
IN ORDER TO GET THE FEEL, PLAY THE SAME PHRASE AGAIN
TRYING TO GET THE SAME FEEL BUT THIS TIME PICKING EVERY
NOTE. IT IS DONE BY PLAYING THE FIRST NOTE OF THE SLURRED
NOTES LOUDER.

THE NOTES IN BRACKETS ARE SLIGHTLY SOFTER

B

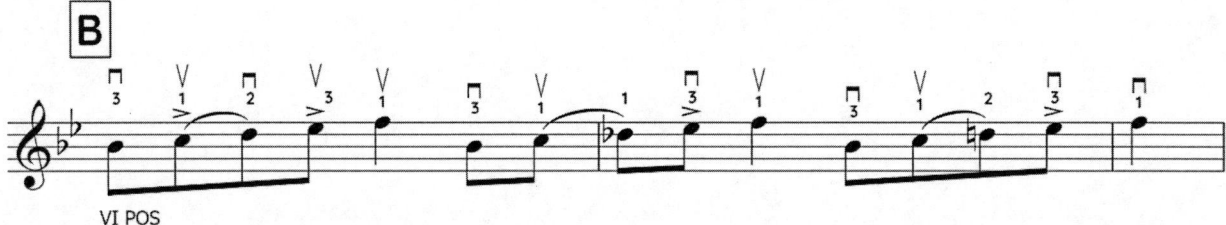

VI POS

NOTICE THAT THIS PHRASE IS 3/4 OVER 4/4

Jimmy Raney's Solo on the Changes of "I Remember You"

Blues (in B♭")

Solo by Jimmy Raney

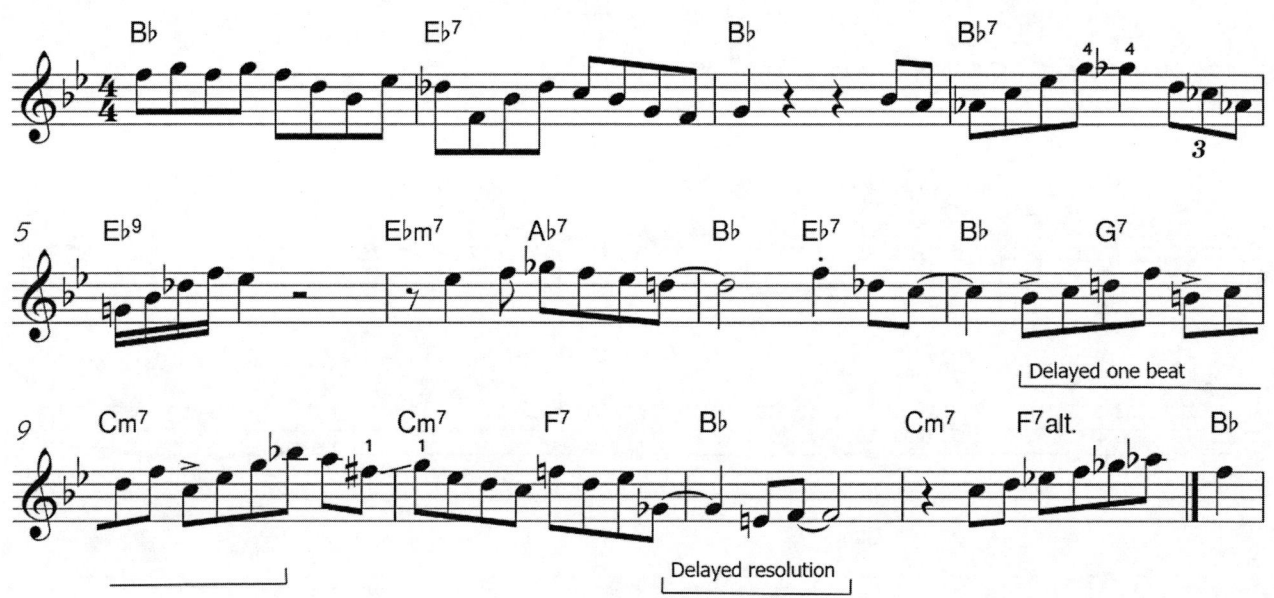

Jimmy Raney's Solo on the Changes of "My Shining Hour"

Blues Exercise

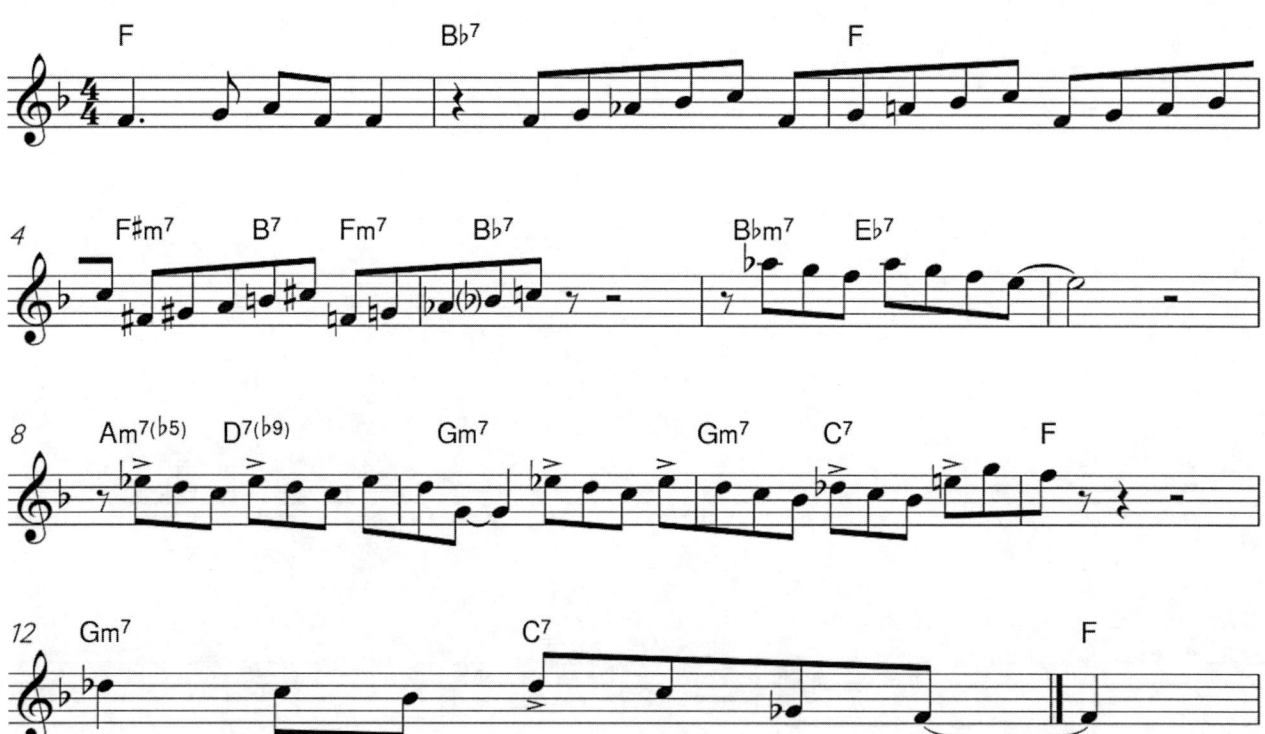

Blues

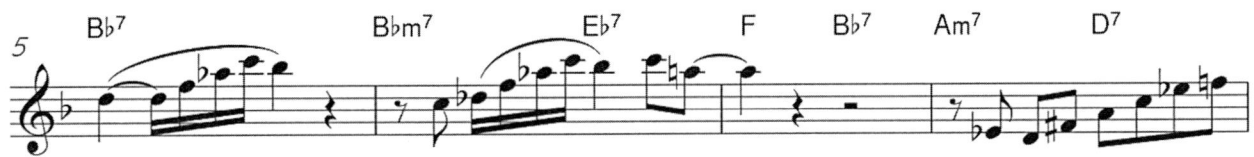

CANON

By Jimmy Raney

EXERCISE

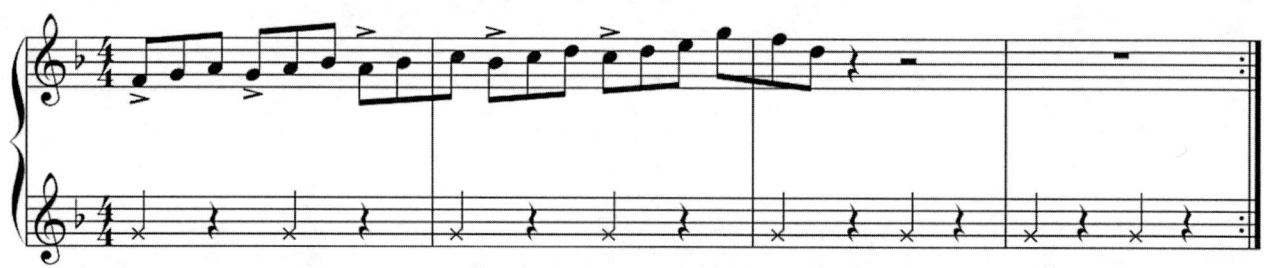

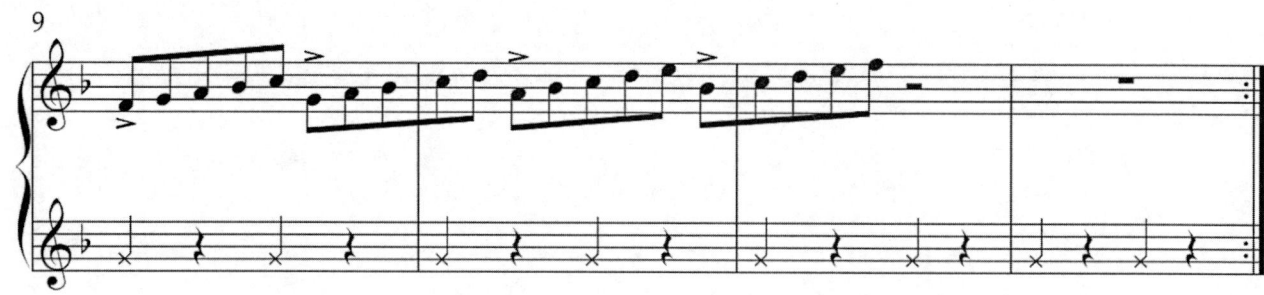

The Sher Music Co. Catalog

BEST-SELLING BOOKS BY MARK LEVINE
The Jazz Theory Book
The Jazz Piano Book
Jazz Piano Masterclass: The Drop 2 Book
How To Voice Standards at the Piano

THE WORLD'S BEST FAKE BOOKS
The New Real Book - Vol. 1 - C, Bb and Eb
The New Real Book - Vol. 2 - C, Bb and Eb
The New Real Book - Vol. 3 - C, Bb, Eb & Bass Clef

The Real Easy Book - Vol. 1 - C, Bb, Eb & Bass Clef
The Real Easy Book - Vol. 2 - C, Bb, Eb & Bass Clef
The Real Easy Book - Vol. 3 - C, Bb, Eb & Bass Clef
The Latin Real Easy Book - C, Bb, Eb & Bass Clef
Drum Supplement for Real Easy Book - Vol. 1

The Standards Real Book - C, Bb and Eb
The Latin Real Book - C, Bb and Eb
The Real Cool Book - Octet charts from the 1950s
The All-Jazz Real Book - with selected audio
The European Real Book - with selected audio
The Best of Sher Music Real Books - C, Bb & Eb
The World's Greatest Fake Book - C only
Jazz Arrangements of Public Domain Songs
The Yellowjackets Songbook - separate parts

LATIN MUSIC BOOKS
Contemporary Latin Jazz Guitar - by Neff Irizarry
Decoding Afro-Cuban Jazz - by Mauleon & Valdes
The Salsa Guidebook - by Rebeca Mauleōn
101 Montunos - by Rebeca Mauleōn
The Latin Bass Book - by Oscar Stagnaro & Chuck Sher
The Latin Real Book - C, Bb, & Eb
The True Cuban Bass - by Carlos del Puerto
The Brazilian Guitar Book - by Nelson Faria
Inside the Brazilian Rhythm Section - Faria/Korman
Conga Drummer's Guidebook - by Michael Spiro
Language of the Masters - by Michael Spiro
Introduction to the Conga Drum DVD - by M. Spiro
Afro-Caribbean Grooves for Drumset - JPhi Fanfant
Afro-Peruvian Percussion Ensemble - H. Morales
Flamenco Improvisation - Vol.1-3 by Enrique Vargas
Muy Caliente! - Afro-Cuban Book & Play-Aong audio
Music of the Arará Savalú Cabildo - Galvin & Spiro

DIGITAL FAKE BOOKS
The New Real Book - Vol.1 - C, Bb & Eb
The Digital Standards Songbook - individual songs with lyrics, plus C, Bb, Eb, High Voice & Low Voice
The Digital Real Book (650 songs from all our books)

THE DIGITAL SONGBOOK SERIES
The Kenny Barron Songbook
The Carla Bley Songbook
The Tom Harrell Songbook
The Oscar Hernandez Songbook
The Alan Pasqua Songbook
The Horace Silver Songbook
The Steve Swallow Songbook
The Ralph Towner Songbook
The Wayne Wallace Songbook
The Kenner Werner Songbook
The Randy Brecker Songbook
The Larry Dunlap Songbook
The Barry Finnerty Songbook
The Benny Golson Songbook
The Steve Khan Songbook
The Doug Morton Songbook
The Andy Narell Songbook
The Enrico Pieranunzi Songbook
The Dave Tull Songbook
The Denny Zeitlin Songbook

FOR STUDENT MUSICIANS
The Real Easy Book - Vol. 1 - C, Bb, Eb & Bass Clef
The Real Easy Book - Vol. 2 - C, Bb, Eb & Bass Clef
The Real Easy Book - Vol. 3 - C, Bb, Eb & Bass Clef
The Latin Real Easy Book - C, Bb, Eb & Bass Clef
Drum Supplement for Real Easy Book - Vol. 1
The Blues Scales - C, Bb, Eb, Bass Clef & Guitar
Rhythm First! - C, Bb, Eb & Bass Clef - by Tom Kamp
Guitarist's Introduction to Jazz - by Randy Vincent
Walking Bassics - by Ed Fuqua
Foundation Exercises for Bass - by Chuck Sher

CDs
Poetry+Jazz: A Magical Marriage - by Chuck Sher
Play-Along CDs for The New Real Book - Vol.1
The Latin Real Book Sampler CD

continued on next page

SHER MUSIC CO. JAZZ METHOD BOOKS
available in both print & digital forms

GUITAR
Jazz Guitar Voicings: The Drop 2 Book
   - Randy Vincent
Three-Note Voicings and Beyond - Randy Vincent
Line Games - Randy Vincent
Jazz Guitar Soloing: The Cellular Approach
   - Randy Vincent
The Guitarist's Introduction to Jazz - Randy Vincent
Contemporary Latin Jazz Guitar - Neff Irizarry

PIANO
The Jazz Piano Book - Mark Levine
Jazz Piano Masterclass: The Drop 2 Book - M. Levine
How To Voice Standards at the Piano - Mark Levine
An Approach to Comping - Vol. 1 - Jeb Patton
An Approach to Comping - Vol. 2 - Jeb Patton
Introduction to Jazz Piano: A Deep Dive - Jeb Patton
Playing for Singers - Mike Greensill
Wisdom of the Hand - Marius Nordal
The Jazz Solos of Chick Corea - Peter Sprague

SAXOPHONE
The Practice Notebooks of Michael Brecker
The Jazz Saxophone Book - Tim Armacost
Logic and Critical Thinking in Jazz Improvisation
   - Vincent Herring

VOICE
The Digital Standards Songbook - individual songs
   with lyrics, plus C, Bb, Eb, High Voice & Low Voice
The Jazz Singer's Guidebook - David Berkman

DRUMS
Syncopation Companion - Bryan Bowman
Inner Drumming - George Marsh
Drum Supplement for Real Easy Book Vol.1 - Alan Hall
Afro-Caribbean Grooves for Drumset - JPhi Fanfant

TRUMPET
New Orleans Trumpet - Jim Thornton
Modern Etudes for Solo Trumpet - Cameron Pearce

BASS
The Improvisor's Bass Method - Chuck Sher
Concepts for Bass Soloing - Marc Johnson & C. Sher
Walking Bassics - Ed Fuqua
Foundation Exercises for Bass - Chuck Sher
Walking Bass Line Construction - F Blues - Bob Sinicrope

JAZZ THEORY AND HARMONY
The Jazz Theory Book - Mark Levine
The Jazz Harmony Book - David Berkman
Forward Motion - Hal Galper
Metaphors for the Musician - Randy Halberstadt
Minor is Major! - Dan Greenblatt
Rhythm Changes Guide - Lukas Gabric
Jazz Scores and Analysis - Vol.1 - Richard Lawn
Jazz Scores and Analysis - Vol. 2 - Richard Lawn
The Blues Scales - C, Bb, Eb, Bass Clef & Guitar
   - Dan Greenblatt
Logic and Critical Thinking in Jazz Improvisation
   - Vincent Herring

PRACTICE GUIDES
The Practice Notebooks of Michael Brecker
Jazz Musician's Guide to Creative Practicing
   - David Berkman
The Serious Jazz Practice Book - Barry Finnerty
The Serious Jazz Book II - Barry Finnerty
Building Solo Lines from Cells - Randy Vincent
365 Days of Practice - Rick Margitza
The Bob Mover Jazz Lexicon - Bob Mover

EAR TRAINING
The Real Easy Ear Training Book - Roberta Radley
Reading, Writing and Rhythmetic - Roberta Radley

RHYTHM SECTION GUIDES
Essential Grooves - Moretti, Stagnaro & Nicholl
Inside the Brazilian Rhythm Section - Nelson Faria
   & Cliff Korman
The Salsa Guidebook - Rebeca Mauleón
Decoding Afro-Cuban Jazz - Mauleón & Valdes

BILINGUAL OR LIBROS EN ESPANOL
101 Montunos - Rebeca Mauleón
Muy Caliente! - Afro-Cuban Book & Play-Along
El Libro del Jazz Piano - Mark Levine
The Latin Real Book - C, Bb and Eb

MISCELLANEOUS
Method for Chromatic Harmonica - Max de Aloe
Jazz Songs for the Student Violinist
   - Kevin Mitchell & Joanne Keefe

*Sign up for our monthly discount newsletter
by writing shermuse@sonic.net*

$32.00
ISBN 978-1-883217-85-3